GUIDE

TO

CHARLESTON

ILLUSTRATED.

BEING A SKETCH OF THE HISTORY OF CHARLESTON, S. C.

WITH SOME ACCOUNT OF

ITS PRESENT CONDITION,

WITH NUMEROUS ENGRAVINGS.

COMPILED BY

ARTHUR MAZYCK, Esq.,

Librarian of the Charleston Library Society.

PRINTED AND PUBLISHED BY

WALKER, EVANS & COGSWELL,

PRINTERS, PUBLISHERS AND ADVERTISING AGENTS.

3 BROAD STREET AND 109 EAST BAY,

CHARLESTON, S. C.

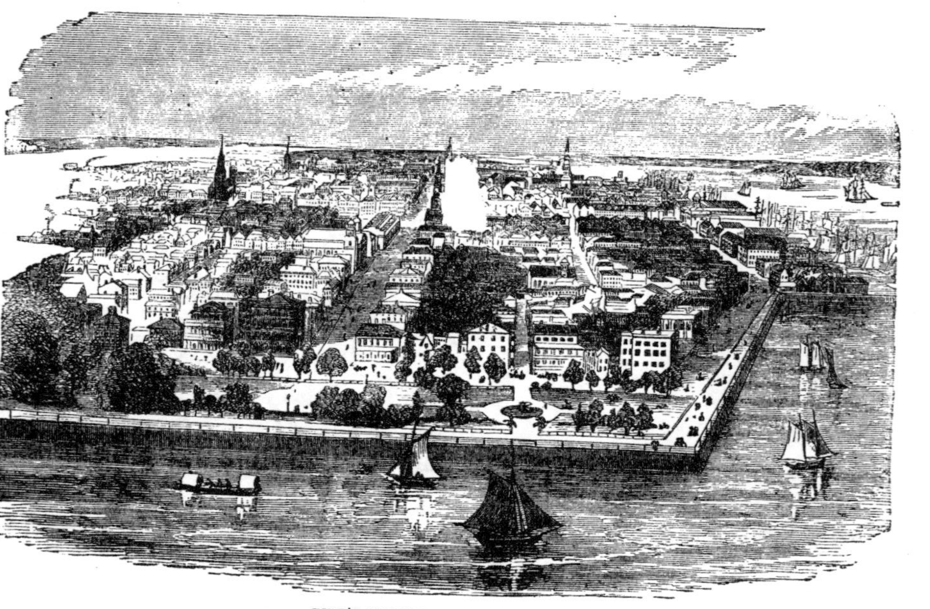

BIRD'S EYE VIEW OF CHARLESTON.

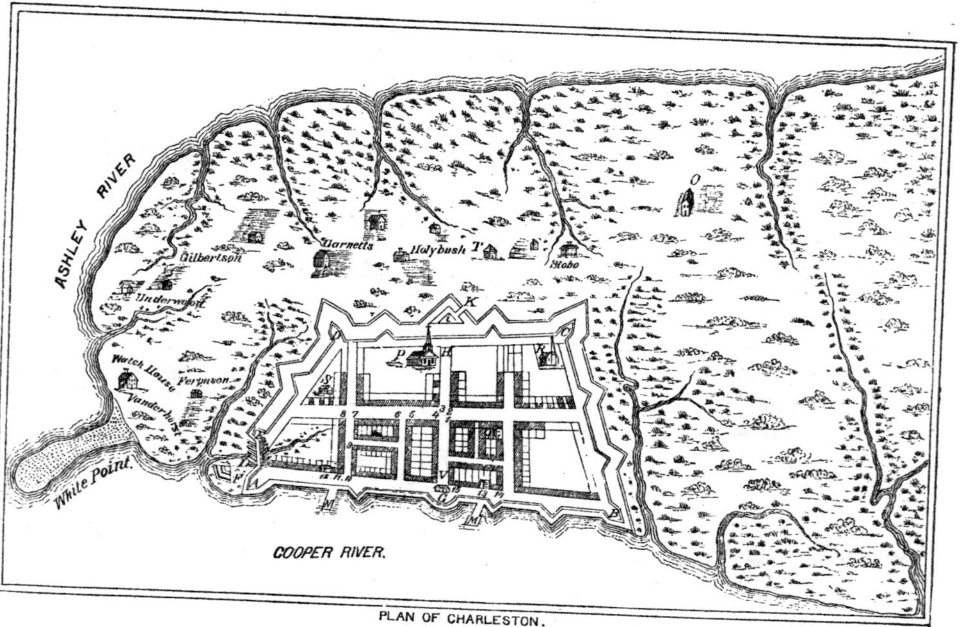

PLAN OF CHARLESTON.

PLAN OF CHARLESTON,

As laid out by John Culpepper, in 1680 with the buildings and fortifications in 1704, by Edward Crisp.

A. Granville's Bastion.
B. Craven's Bastion.
C. Carteret's Bastion.
D. Colleton Bastion.
E Ashley Bastion.
F. Blake's Bastion.
G. Half Moon Bastion.
H. Drawbridge.
I· Johnson's.
K Drawbridge.
L. Palisades.
M. Rhett's Bridge.
N. K. L. Smith's Bridge.
O. Minister's House.
P. English Church.
Q. French Church.
R Independent Church.
S. Anabaptist Church.
T. Quaker Meeting House.
V. Court of Guards.
W. First Rice Patch in Carolina.
1. Pasquero and Garret's House.
2. Landsack's House.
3. John Crosskey's House.
4. Chevalier's House.
5. George Logan's House.
6. Poinsett's House.
7. Ellicott's House.
8. Starling's House.
9. M. Boone's House.
10. Tradd's House.
11. Nat. Law's House.
12. Landgrave Smith's House.
13. Col. Rhett's House.
14 Ben. Skenking's House.
15. Sindery's House.

Photo. by Barnard. *Eng. by Photo. Eng. Co., N. Y.*

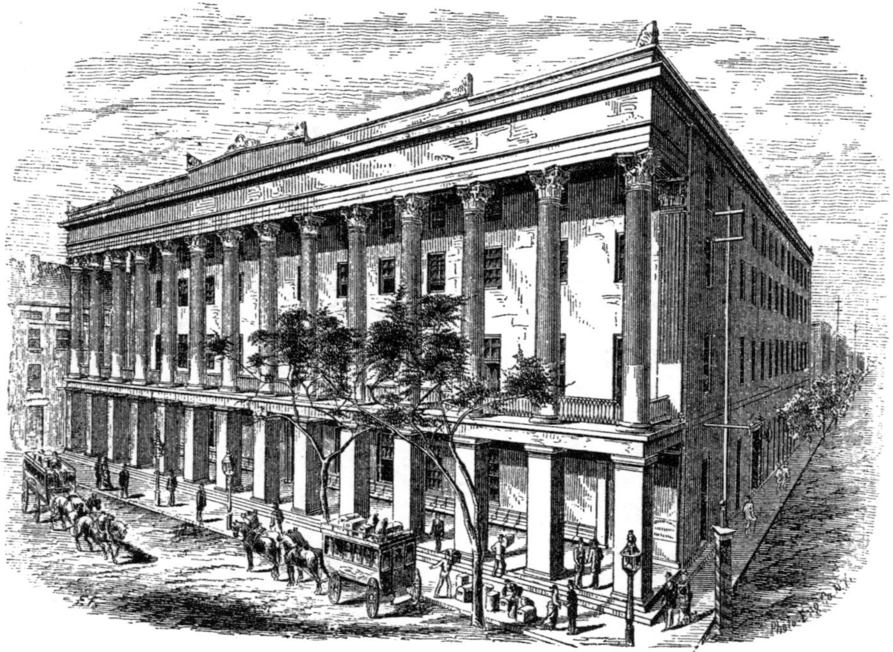

Photo. by Barnard.

CHARLESTON HOTEL.

Eng. by Photo. Eng. Co., N. Y.

Photo. by Barnard. *Eng. by Photo. Eng. Co., N. Y.*

PRIVATE RESIDENCE OF GEO. W. WILLIAMS, ESQ.

CONTENTS.

Photo. by Barnard. *Eng. by Photo. Eng. Co., N. Y.*

RUINS OF THE CATHEDRAL.

DESCRIPTION

OF

CHARLESTON, S. C.

Beautiful as a dream, tinged with romance, consecrated by tradition, glorified by history, rising from the very bosom of the waves, like a fairy city created by the enchanter's wand, Charleston affords a fit theme for poet, novelist, historian, and tourist. The family names of the Cavaliers and Huguenots still live to tell of the origin of the people; Moultrie still frowns above the bay that resounded to the first cannon of the first revolution a hundred years ago; grim visaged Sumter stands a melancholy witness of heroic deeds of later times. These are the three salient points that strike the mind as the fabric of her history is scanned; but the Indian wars, the French war, the Spanish invasion, the Mexican war, political contests without number, serve to fill in the sketch, like minor turrets on the great wall of peaceful years, which, after all, is, indeed, the basis and the body of the structure. Before turning back to trace the story here so dimly outlined, let us take a glance at

THE CITY AS IT IS.

Charleston is situated on a tongue of land between the Ashley and the Cooper Rivers, and at the head of an extensive, yet land-locked bay, affording the safest and most commodious harbor on the Atlantic coast. It is the only city on the American Continent from which the ocean can be seen. The bay is a beautiful sheet of water, three miles wide, and at the city forty feet deep, affording ample sea room for the commerce of the world. Around the neck of this bay lies a bead-work of rich islands, producing the premium cotton and rice of the world, with their waters abounding in fish and game. To the back of the city, within ten miles, lie truck farms producing four crops per annum, and beyond these the inexhaustible phosphate beds of untold fertilizing wealth.

Spread a map before you, and pass your eye from St. Louis to Charleston, S. C., and you will trace the *shortest* road to the ocean, and almost a bee-line along the Southern Pacific Railroad, affording the shortest line to California, tapping the great valleys of the West, intersecting the grain-growing and cattle-raising States, cutting the great cotton belt, and branching off to all the rich marts of trade and splendid cities along the line. If it be the fixed law of commerce to take the shortest and cheapest route, Charleston has no rival, and opens the finest sea-gate to the

West on the American Continent. Two lines of railroad connect the city with the North and South, and only a few connecting links are wanting to give us three competing lines to the West, and these are being rapidly supplied by energetic men. Railroads in the city run down to the wharves and deliver produce alongside the shipping, affording thereby a prompt and safe landing of goods. The fruit, sugar, coffee, tobacco, and tropical productions of Cuba, the West Indies, and South America, come directly to our port in large shipments, and that the year round. Our harbor is never frozen ; steamers and railroads never obstructed, delaying transportation and increasing expenses. Steamers ply weekly, or more frequently, from this port to New York, Philadelphia, Boston, Baltimore, Savannah, and other places. From early spring, in February, to the fall, they supply the North with vegetables in great variety and of unsurpassed quality. Strawberries, peas, beans, potatoes, squashes, cucumbers, tomatoes, melons, cabbage, and other table plants, are shipped in immense quantities from farms adjacent to the city. Thousands of tons of phosphate, both in crude rock and manipulated, were sent off last season, and some of it was exported to Europe.

The city is about three miles long from the Battery to the Forks of the road, and about two miles wide at the widest points, and half a mile at the narrowest. The streets are irregular and run around in quite a labyrinthian fashion, cutting up the town into all sorts of quadrangles, and seeming at first to make its topography quite a puzzle; but if a stranger will fix in his memory Rutledge, Meeting, King, Church, and East Bay streets, running up and down, and Broad, Wentworth, Calhoun, and Cannon streets, running across, he will soon find himself able to solve, without assistance, all problems as to locality and distance. King street is generally known as the fashionable promenade and shopping street; Meeting street as the locality for the jobbing trade in dry goods, clothing, shoes, crockery, etc.; East Bay as the street for grocers, ship chandlers, etc.; and Broad street for banks, lawyers, and brokers. In King street, above Queen street, on both sides, and just below it on the east side, are a number of stores, erected since the war, and filling up almost completely the ugly gap in the street made by the great fire of 1861. Above this, again, the stores improve in size and appearance, and are occupied by the more important retail dealers, until you reach Calhoun street. Above that you have about two miles of small stores, with here and there a really fine store. The business part of Meeting street is between Wentworth and Market streets, supplementing itself with Hayne street, a short street running from Meeting to Church street, and on which are establishments of some of the largest houses in the city. The grocery business, on East Bay, extends from Market street to Broad street. The banks cluster around the corner of East Bay and Broad streets, while the lawyers and brokers stretch along Broad street from East Bay to Meeting street. The finest residences are to be seen on East and South Battery,

Meeting street, below Broad street, Rutledge street and Avenue, and the west end of Wentworth street.

The offices of the factors, and the seat of the cotton trade, the leading business in the city, are on the wharves, on the eastern side of the city, below Market street. The population of Charleston, according to the United States census for 1870, was forty-eight thousand nine hundred and fifty-six; of these twenty-six thousand two hundred and seven were whites, and twenty-two thousand seven hundred and forty-nine were blacks or colored. The white population is now probably several thousand larger, while the colored population is at a stand-still, or has increased very little. The weekly bills of mortality show a much larger proportion of deaths among the colored population than among the whites, and if the white population is alone considered, Charleston can be shown to be one of the healthiest cities in the United States.

In a commercial and business point of view, Charleston is the only city between Baltimore and New Orleans that has the geographical position to command trade and prosperity. Nearer than any other Atlantic port to the great grain States of the North-west, the natural terminus of any Southern Pacific railroad, with no seaport of any consequence nearer to it on the north than Norfolk, nor on the south than New Orleans, it becomes necessarily the emporium of direct trade between the South and Europe, and of the coast trade between the South and the Northern and Eastern States. Manufactures in va-

NEW CUSTOM HOUSE.

rious branches have been undertaken since the war, and have met with wonderful success. A more detailed account of the commerce of the City, as well as of the jobbing trade, and various manufacturing establishments, hotels, churches, places of amusement, etc., will be given in another part of the book, but enough has been said at present as an introduction to the following historical sketch.

HISTORICAL SKETCH

OF

CHARLESTON, S. C.

THE City of Charleston owes its origin to a party of English Colonists, sent over by the Lords Proprietors, under Col. William Sayle, in the year 1669. These Proprietors were Edward, Earl of Clarendon; George, Duke of Albemarle; William, Lord Craven; John, Lord Berkley; Anthony, Lord Ashley; Sir George Carteret; Sir William Berkley, and Sir John Colleton, to whom an extensive grant of lands in America, including the whole of the Carolinas, had been made in 1663, by Charles II.

Several expeditions were sent out by them, but that under Col. Sayle was the first to make a permanent settlement. The Colonists landed first at Port Royal, attracted thither by its fine harbor, but it was too near the Spanish settlements in Florida, and the Indian tribes allied with the Spaniards, for the peace or safety of the Colony, and they soon determined to move further up the coast. Leaving between themselves and their enemies the several rivers and bays which indent the coast of Carolina between Port Royal and Charleston, they selected as the site of their town a spot on the west bank of the Ashley, about three miles above the present city, and called it, in honor of the King, Charles Town.

In a little while it was found that the situation of the town was inconvenient for shipping, and by degrees the inhabitants began to establish themselves nearer the sea.

The point formed by the confluence of the Ashley and Cooper Rivers, and known as Oyster Point, was low and marshy, and cut up by numerous creeks, but there was sufficient high ground on the Cooper River side to afford room for a settlement, and in the course of a few years (1677) there were enough houses built upon it to need some designation, and it was called by the rather humble title of Oyster Point Town.

In 1680, so large a majority of the people had removed to this spot that it was formally made the seat of government, and called New Charles Town. Two years later the former settlement was virtually abandoned, and the new one became the only Charles Town. It was at that time declared a port of entry, and in 1685 a Collector was appointed. The city was incorporated under its present name of Charleston, by the State Legislature, in 1783.

Of the first settlement on the Ashley there is now scarcely a trace remaining; the creek immediately below it is called Old Town Creek, and a half-filled ditch is sometimes pointed out as having formed part of the works for the defence of the town; but there is nothing to show on what plan it was laid out, or what was its extent or character.

On looking at any early plan of our present City we are hardly surprised that it should not have been at first selected as the site upon which to build, and we cannot too greatly admire the energy and patience of the men who triumphed over the difficulties which nature interposed, and laid the foundations of the City destined to play so important a part in the history of America.

We select as our illustration (*see frontispiece*) the plan from a survey made by Edward Crisp, in 1704, which will show the topography of the town and surrounding country, and give some idea of what were the difficulties to which we have alluded. In the space now included between Water and Calhoun streets there were no less than ten large creeks, with numerous branches, besides several ponds and low marshy spots. The town at that period was bounded on the south by a creek which occupied the site of Water street, and which was then or soon after known as Vanderhorst's Creek; on the north by another large creek, where the market now is; on the east by Cooper River, the shore of which was much further in than it now is, covering all the land now occupied by the offices and warehouses on the east side of East Bay street, while the western boundary was just a little beyond Meeting street.

Within the first year thirty houses were built, mostly of wood. We will mention a few of those laid down on the map, so as to show the principal localities first settled upon.

The intersection of Broad and Church streets may be taken as the central spot of the town; the corners being occupied, respectively, as follows:

1. Pasquero and Garrett's house, north-east corner, the site now occupied by Messrs. Klinck, Wickenberg & Co.

2. Landsack's house, north-west corner, now occupied by the building of the Charleston Library Society.

3. John Croskey's house, south-west corner, now occupied by the store of Messrs. Jno. Paul & Co.

4. Chevelier's house, south-east corner, site now occupied by a building owned by C. Plenge.

Tradd's house stood on the north-west corner of Tradd and East Bay streets. The site was afterwards owned by Gen. Pinckney.

Landgrave Thomas Smith's house was on the south-west corner of East Bay and Longitude lane. On the lot in rear of this house the first rice ever raised in Carolina was planted, about the year 1693. The last traces of the old settlement are now gone, and the extensive buildings of the Palmetto Cotton Press Company are being erected on the land.

Col. Rhett's house was on the west side of the Bay, near Unity alley, on the site now occupied by the Planters' and Mechanics' Bank.

On the east side of Bay street, directly opposite Broad street was the Court of Guards or Garrison.

The Public Market was at the western limit of the town, where the City Hall now stands.

ST. MICHAEL'S.

The English Church (St. Philip's) was built 1681-2, on the south-east corner of Broad and Meeting streets, the site now occupied by St. Michael's Church.

The French Church (Huguenot) was on the lot of

land occupied by the present French Protestant Church.

The Independent Church was on the east side of Meeting street, on the spot now marked by the ruins of the Circular Church ; and the Baptist, or Anabaptist, was on the west side of Church street, a little above Water, where the Baptist Church now stands.

There was also a Quaker meeting house, but that was outside of the limits of the town, and stood on a lot on the east side of King street, a few doors below Queen.

The site of the present Court House was a large pond, but this was probably artificial, being caused by the digging of several deep trenches for defence against a threatened invasion of the Indians in 1703. It was not drained until 1756.

The land was deeply indented at the foot of Queen street, forming a kind of natural dock, whence its name at that time of Dock street.

Dr. Ramsay in his history mentions that the north end of Union street (now State street) was planted with rice as late as 1755.

At the extreme point of the Peninsula outside of the town, on the point called Oyster Point, and afterwards White Point, was the old Watch House.

The town consisted in all of eight streets and one alley, viz : Tradd, Elliott, Broad, and Queen, running east and west from Bay street to Church and Meeting ; and Bay, Union, Church and Meeting streets, and Bedon's alley, running north and south.

For protection against enemies from abroad as well

as the Indians, who frequently threatened the safety of the inhabitants, the town was fortified by bastions at the salient points, connected by earthworks.

Ashley's bastion stood on the northern margin of Vanderhorst's creek (Water street); to the east of this, across the creek, was Granville's bastion, while south-east of the latter, on the hardage, or beach, was a detached battery, or bastion, called Blake's bastion.

Craven's bastion was on the southern margin of the creek which formed the upper boundary of the town, that is about the corner of East Bay and Market streets. Carteret's was on a line with it and Meeting street, and Colleton's at the point where Vanderhorst's creek crossed Meeting street, *i. e.* at Price's alley. At each end of Broad street was a half-moon, or detached bastion, that at the western extremity being called Johnson's half-moon.

Within these limits the town was comprehended until the year 1743, by which time it had outgrown its limits, and a new survey was made, which added several squares. The northern boundary was extended to a line near Beaufain street, continued from river to river, and the western to the Ashley. Among the principal streets, added at this time, were Lamboll, Legare, Orange, and Friend, below Broad street, and Mazyck, Archdale, Clifford, Beresford, and Magazine, above it. By degrees these boundaries extended themselves and new streets and squares were added, which were from time to time included in the municipality.

Such was the early topography of the city of

Charleston, which we have described in order that it may be seen how the city gradually extended itself to its present limits.

As to the inhabitants, we have seen that the first settlers were Englishmen. They were of various classes and conditions of life; some of them Cavaliers, friends or connexions of the Lords Proprietors, whom an adventurous spirit led to visit the new world; others, men of lower degree, seeking their fortunes under circumstances of greater freedom than the condition of affairs in Great Britain at that time permitted.

They were joined in the years 1685 and 1686 by a number of Huguenots, whom the revocation of the edict of Nantz had driven from France, and these soon formed an important part of the population. A few brought money with them and were able at once to enter into commerce and to become landholders. All of them were trained to habits of industry, and the strict, almost austere nature of their religion, and the trials which they had gone through, made them earnest, hard-working men, well fitted to combat the many difficulties and disappointments incident to the settlement of a wild and untried country.

Immigrants from other parts of the world also, for various reasons, found their way to the new town. These different elements naturally took some time to settle into a state of harmony. The Cavaliers and the Puritans could not easily forget their old feuds, and the French were for a long time regarded as aliens, and debarred from all political privileges.

But the common dangers and labors which they

had to undergo together, and the necessity of combined action, in time caused their differences to be forgotten and all worked together for the general good.

South Carolina, however, showed a revolutionary spirit very early. We have seen that the province was under the exclusive control of the Lords Proprietors; they appointed the governors, who administered the laws as laid down in constitutions, framed by them or under their direction, the most famous of which was that said to have been constructed by the philosopher, John Locke. It was in this that provision was made for certain titles of nobility, among them that of Landgrave, which we have seen applied to Mr. Thomas Smith.

From a very early period difficulties were continually arising between the people and their rulers; the various grounds of difference were too numerous, and too complex, to set down here. It is sufficient to observe that the Proprietors away in England could neither understand nor sympathize with the condition of the colonists here, and while on the one hand they were unable or unwilling to fulfil many of their pledges to the crown and to the people of the colony, on the other they were frequently disposed to usurp greater powers than were granted to them. At length in the year 1719, the people formed a secret scheme for throwing off the government of the Proprietors, and putting themselves directly under that of the British Crown, and, in December of that year, they formally notified the Governor, Robert Johnson, of their intention. Johnson of course endeavored to maintain his position, but the people standing firm, he perceived that resistance would be useless.

They chose James Moore as their governor, subject to the direct authority of the British Government.

Having thus briefly sketched the first settlement of our City, we turn naturally to those landmarks which remain either in their original form, or so changed as to illustrate its present condition ; and first among these, in point of time, as well as on account of its many interesting associations comes

ST. PHILIP'S CHURCH.

In the original plan of Charles Town, a lot was set apart for a church, and upon this lot, at the south-east corner of Broad and Meeting streets, the site of the present St. Michael's, the first Episcopal Church in the province, was built in 1681–82. It was usually called the English Church, but its distinctive name was St. Philip's. We learn that it was built of black cypress, on a brick foundation, but not much is known of the particulars of its appearance. In March, 1710–11, an Act of Assembly was passed for the building of a new church of brick, the one just referred to having begun to decay, and being rather too small for the increased size of the congregation. This second church was built on the site occupied by the present one on the east side of Church street, a short distance above Queen ; it was first opened for divine service in 1723, but was not entirely finished until

ST. PHILIP'S CHURCH.

1727; in fact, the steeple was never carried to the height originally intended, thus marring the effect of the architecture. It was, notwithstanding this, a very elegant and imposing building, and continued for upwards of a hundred years, the pride and admiration of all who were connected with it.

On Sunday morning, February 15, 1835, a fire broke out in some buildings to the north of the Church, and the wind blowing strongly from that direction, sparks were lodged in the wood work of the steeple, which soon caught, and in a very short time the whole building was so enveloped in the flames that all the efforts of the citizens who flocked to the scene were unavailing, and it was completely destroyed, to the great grief of the entire community as well as of its own congregation.

Preparations were immediately made to repair the loss, and on the 12th November of the same year the corner stone of the present Church was laid, with appropriate ceremonies, on the same site.

Service was first held in it on the 3rd May, 1838, and it was consecrated by Bishop Bowen, on the 9th November of the same year. It is a very beautiful edifice, with a graceful spire on the western extremity, rising two hundred feet; the interior, with its lofty arched roof, profusely ornamented and supported by perfect Corinthian columns, is remarkable for the elegance and correctness of its architecture. It was furnished with an excellent chime of bells, but these were broken up and cast into cannon during the late war, and as yet the means of the Church have not been sufficient to replace them. The clock in the steeple has long been disused.

There are two cemeteries attached to the Church, one immediately around it, and the other across

Church street, extending back to the cemetery of the Independent Church. Near the centre of this second cemetery stands a square brick tomb, covered with a plain marble slab, where rest the remains of Calhoun.

ST. MICHAEL'S CHURCH.

The history of St. Michael's Church is so intimately associated with that of St. Philip's that, although it does not follow in strict chronological order, we naturally look next for it.

An Act of Assembly, passed June 14, 1751, divided the town into two Parishes; all north of Broad street to be called St. Philip's, and all south of it St. Michael's. The same Act directed the building of a Church on the site lately occupied by St. Philip's, at the south-east corner of Broad and Meeting streets. The South Carolina Gazette, of February 22, 1752, states that the corner stone of the new Church was laid with much ceremony, on the 17th of that month; it further mentions that "this Church will be built on the plan of one of Mr. Gibson's designs," but nothing more is known of the architect. The entire cost of construction was only $32,755.87. It is of brick, rough cast, and is now colored white. The outside dimensions are, length one hundred and thirty feet; width sixty feet; the steeple is one hundred and eighty feet in height, and was for a long time unsurpassed for its architectural beauty by any in America. There is a peculiar repose and stability about the entire structure, which never fails to im-

Photo. by Barnard. *Eng. by Photo. Eng. Co., N. Y.*

ST. MICHAEL'S CHURCH, (LOOKING NORTH.)

press the beholder. The steeple is a very prominent landmark, and can be seen at sea for several miles. During the late war the greater part of the shells from the Federal batteries, on Morris Island, were aimed directly at it, but strange to say it was not once struck. The body of the Church was several times struck, but without very serious injury.

The Church was first opened for divine worship

February 1, 1761. The bells and clock were imported from England in 1764, and the organ in 1768 The history of these bells is peculiarly interesting. When the British evacuated Charleston, in December, 1782, Major Traille, of the Royal Artillery, seized the bells on the pretence that they were a military perquisite. The citizens applied for them on the ground that they had been purchased by private subscription, and Sir Guy Carleton issued an order for their restoration, but they had already been shipped to England, where they were sold and purchased by a Mr. Ryhineu, and reshipped. They arrived in Charleston in November, 1783, and were immediately taken possession of and replaced in the belfry.

In 1861 they were removed to Columbia for safety, and when that city was burned by Sherman, they were so much injured by fire as to be rendered entirely useless; two of them were stolen and could never be recovered.

In the Spring of 1866, they were again sent to England to be recast; this was done by the successors of the firm that had made them a hundred years before, from the same patterns, and on the 18th February, 1867, the eight bells, as nearly identical as possible with the original ones, were landed in Charleston; they were detained in the Custom House stores for some time, until arrangements could be made for the payment of the very heavy duty, amounting to upwards of two thousand dollars, but on the 21st March, 1867, they were again placed in the steeple, and the familiar chimes once more rang

Photo. by Barnard. *Eng. by Photo. Eng. Co., N. Y.*

ST. MICHAEL'S CHURCH, LOOKING SOUTH, WITH CITY HALL IN FOREGROUND.

out. No sound appeals so touchingly to the heart of a Charlestonian as these old bells, and their return was a source of deep emotion.

The Cemetery of St. Michael's extends on the south to St. Michael's Alley, and in rear of the Church to the Mansion House lot; in it are interred the remains of many of Charleston's most honored citizens.

We turn next to the

EXCHANGE, OR POST OFFICE.

We have seen that the old Court of Guards stood on the east side of the Bay, facing Broad street. In

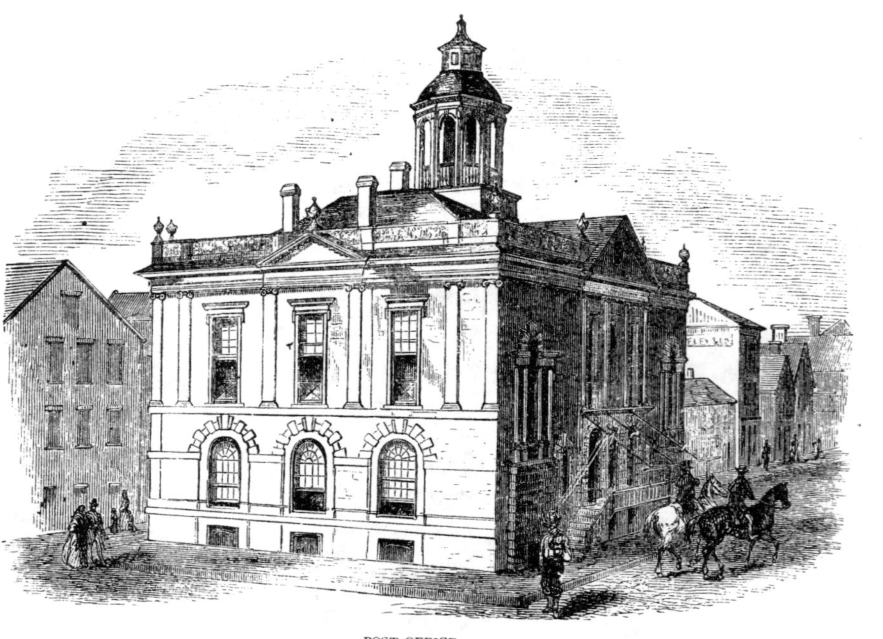

POST OFFICE.

1761, an Act of Assembly was passed for the erection on this site of an Exchange, the contract for building it given to Messrs. Peter and John A. Horlbeck, ancestors of the present family of that name, and the cost was fixed at £44,016 16s. 8d., gold. Most of the material used was brought from England. When completed it became the general business mart of Charleston, and so continued for many years. During the occupation of the city by the British, its lower floors were used as a prison, and in one of the rooms Col. Isaac Hayne was confined and thence taken to execution.

Afterwards the vaults were used as vendue stores, until the building of the present Vendue Range, and the rest of the building as Post Office and Custom House. The situation becoming unsafe in the late war, it was deserted, and fell almost to ruin; but it has since been refitted, the Post Office and Custom House re-established in it, and the building now presents a very imposing appearance.

The front was originally on the east side, and wings extended out on East Bay, but as these obstructed the street they were taken down and the front changed to the western side.

The South Carolina Society, whose hall is represented in our illustration along with St. Michael's Church, deserves mention, as one of the earliest benevolent institutions in this country, and one which has to the present day continued its good work. It originated in the year 1737, with a few gentlemen, who used to meet once a week, at a tavern at the north-east corner of Broad and Church streets; each

Photo. by Barnard. *Eng. by Photo. Eng. Co., N. Y.*

SOUTH CAROLINA SOCIETY HALL.

contributed a small sum (two bits, or four half-pence) for charitable purposes, and the Society was for some time known as the Two-Bit Club. It was incorporated in 1751, under the name of the South Carolina Society, and increased so rapidly, that in 1770, it had three hundred and sixty members, and a capital of £7,500 sterling.

The Society continued to prosper, and much good was effected by giving aid to the needy families of deceased members, and educating their children. For some years a school was kept up under its auspices, but this was superseded by the public schools of the City. In common with all such institutions, it met with heavy losses in the late war, but still continues to aid its pensioners.

The present hall is situated on the east side of Meeting street, a short distance south of St. Michael's Church. It is a substantial structure of two stories, on a high basement. The second story contains a fine hall, on the walls of which are marble tablets, with the names of persons who have made donations or bequests to the Society. On the front of the colonade, which extends over the sidewalk, the seal of the Society is represented, consisting of a hand holding an olive branch, with the legend "*Posteritati.*"

The St. Andrew's Society, which also expended a considerable amount in charity, was founded in 1729, and is the oldest society in Charleston. It had accumulated a fund, and owned a fine hall in Broad Street, near the Cathedral. This was destroyed in the fire of December, 1861, and the Society has not yet recovered from the severe losses sustained then and during the war.

The German Friendly Society, established in 1766, and incorporated in 1791, also uses its funds for educational and charitable purposes.

The first religious charitable society in America was "The Society for the Relief of the Widows and Orphans of the Clergy of the Protestant Episcopal Church in South Carolina," which was established in Charleston in 1762, and which, notwithstanding the two revolutions it has passed through, continues still the support of many families of clergymen.

The Charleston Library Society was the earliest association of its kind in Charleston, and the third in the United States. It was organized in 1748, by seventeen young gentlemen, who desired to obtain some of the current literature from England. They soon associated others with them, and, after some difficulties, a charter was obtained in 1754, under the name of the Charles Town Library Society. It increased in numbers and wealth, and in spite of the heavy loss sustained by the fire of 1778, acquired an extremely valuable collection of books. These were kept at first at the residence or office of the librarian, and afterwards in the third story of the State House (now the Court House). In 1835 the Society purchased its present building, at the north-west corner of Broad and Church streets. This building was erected for the South Carolina Bank, and was occupied by it for some years. It is massively built of red brick, faced with white marble, and presents a square front on Broad street, with wings extending from the north-east and north-west corners. The number of volumes was about twenty thousand in 1860, and the Society was in a flourishing condition. During the war the greater part of the books, including the most valuable works, was removed to Columbia for safety, but a considerable number were left in the building, and were entirely destroyed. After the war the Society was re-organized, and, in 1874, the Apprentices' Library Society was merged in it, bring-

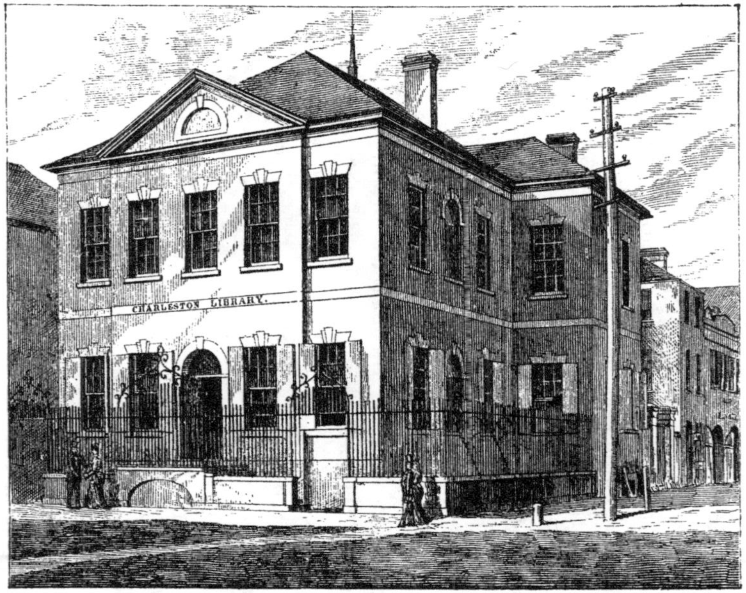

Photo. by Barnard. *Eng. by Photo. Eng. Co., N. Y.*

CHARLESTON LIBRARY.

ing a large accession of members and some funds. The condition of the Society now is very promising. In the value of its collection it ranks first in the South, and efforts are now being made to render it more popular and attractive, by large additions of current literature. A curious story is told in connection with this building. While it was occupied by the Bank, in 1802, an attempt was made by a man named Withers to enter the vaults under the building, by cutting through from beneath. To do this he entered the drain on the opposite side of the street, and for three months continued to dig his way towards the building. At length his confederate, a boy, was observed, by one of the clerks in a neighboring store, in the act of letting down food through the drain, and he was captured. He was arraigned for the attempt to rob, but not having accomplished his design, was released. The most remarkable fact is that his health is said not to have suffered at all from his long confinement under ground.

The Court House stands at the north-west corner of Broad and Meeting streets, on the site of the old State House. After that was destroyed by fire in 1788, and the Legislature had removed its sittings to Columbia, the present building was erected on the same foundation, and became the Charleston Court House, and is one of the best specimens of architecture in the city. It is built of brick, faced so as to resemble stone ; the principal front is on Broad street, and presents a central projection, formed by a screen of columns raised on a rustic arcade, the whole rising

Photo. by Barnard. *Eng. by Photo. Eng. Co., N. Y.*

COURT HOUSE.

the entire height of the building. The first floor comprises a large central hall, and the rooms of the officers of the court; from the hall a broad staircase leads to the second floor, the western portion of which is the present court room; the eastern, formerly the Equity Court room, is now used as the clerk's office and depository of the books of the court; the third floor contains the jury rooms.

On the north-east corner of Broad and Meeting streets is the City Hall; this building was erected for the United States Bank, and was purchased by the City when the Bank was removed from Charleston, with the money received from the sale of the Exchange to the United States Government.

Though somewhat defective in architecture, it is a very imposing building; the front is on Broad street, and a double flight of marble steps leads to the first floor, which stands upon a high basement; the whole front of this floor is a large hall, paved with marble, in which the City Court is held; in the rear are the offices of the City Treasurer and Assessor, and the staircase leading to the second floor, which is occupied by the Council Chamber, and offices of the Mayor, and other city officials. The Council Chamber is handsomely furnished, and contains full length portraits of several distinguished citizens. The building stands in an open square, planted with shade trees. The north-west corner of this square is occupied by the Fire-proof Building, a massive structure entirely protected against damage by fire; its most valuable contents are the records of the Mesne Conveyance office, and the office of the Judge of Probates. We have already described St. Michael's Church, which stands on the south-east corner of Broad and Meeting streets; the south-west corner is occupied by the Guard House, a plain substantial building, with a colonade extending over the side walk on Broad street; the City Police are quartered in it, and it is also used for the temporary confinement of prisoners arrested by them.

As early as 1783, a Chamber of Commerce was established in Charleston; but there are no records of its proceedings remaining, and it appears to have fallen into entire disuse and oblivion. In 1823, combined action of the merchants of the city becoming necessary in consequence of the action of the Legislature in relation to certain taxes, etc., meetings

Photo. by Barnard. *Eng. by Photo. Eng. Co., N. Y.*

CHAMBER OF COMMERCE.

were held, the result of which was the re-establishment of the Chamber, and since that time it has continued a well organized body, and, especially in the past few years, has exercised a very powerful influence on the commerce of Charleston; many questions are settled. by it, which might otherwise lead to tedious litigation; valuable statistical reports are prepared and published, internal improvements are suggested and aided, and numerous other benefits are derived by the city from this body, which comprises among its active members the most prominent business men in the community. The Chamber at present occupies the second and third floors of a handsome building at the north-west corner of Broad and East Bay streets; it has a commodious reading room, supplied with the leading American and foreign papers and periodicals, and club rooms, and restaurant, for the use of the members.

The buildings and associations which we have described belong to Charleston before the Revolution, and while it is not proposed to offer these descriptions according to an exact chronological arrangement, yet it is well so to group them as to associate them with the several divisions into which the history of the city naturally falls.

We come now to the period of the Revolution. At this time Charleston was in a very prosperous condition—commerce was flourishing, and the interior of the State was gradually filling up and forming, as it were, a background for the metropolis. All fears from the neighboring Spaniards and Indians were removed, and peace reigned at home and abroad.

The relations with the mother country were friendly, and the people were very loyal to the British Government; it was, therefore, from no spirit of discontent or restiessness that the inhabitants commenced their resistance to that government, but from a sense of the duty which rested on them to oppose what they considered unjust encroachments of their rights as subjects.

The first open cause of difficulty occurred, as is well known, on the passage of the stamp act in 1765; the resistance of all the American Colonies brought about the repeal of this in the following year. In 1767, taxes were laid on glass, paper, tea, and painters' colors; the colonists petitioned for their removal, and formed associations among themselves, pledged not to import those articles. The taxes were removed, except that of threepence a pound on tea, upon which the colonists promptly bound themselves to use no more of it. In 1773, the famous tea affair occurred; the East India Company sent large cargoes into the various American ports, in hopes that, as the payment of the tax would not be made directly to the British Government, but through them, it might meet with a sale, but the colonists perceived the evasion, and would have none of it; in Charles Town it was stored in cellars, and the consignees were prohibited from offering it for sale.

On the 6th of July, 1774, a large meeting was held in Charles Town, composed of persons from all parts of the province, and the action of the British Government, in relation especially to Massachusetts, was discussed and resolutions adopted, looking to a combination of the several colonies to secure themselves against a continuance of such action. Henry Middleton, John Rutledge, Christopher Gadsden, Thomas

Lynch, and Edward Rutledge, were appointed deputies to represent the province in a convention of the colonies. The action of that convention, and of the subsequent Congress, belong to the general history of the country; it is sufficient to observe that the people of Charleston and of Carolina, generally, promptly acquiesced in it, and prepared themselves for armed resistance to the power of Great Britain. Active hostilities commenced in South Carolina on the 12th November, 1775, when two royal armed vessels, the Tamar and the Cherokee, opened fire on the schooner Defence, Captain Tufts, which was engaged in protecting the sinking of hulks across Hog Island Channel. The defence returned the fire, but there was no loss on either side. Col. William Moultrie having taken possession, with a small force, of Haddrell's Point, mounted a few pieces of heavy artillery there, and with a well directed fire, induced the British vessels to put to sea.

The first blood was shed in the memorable battle of Fort Moultrie, on the 28th of June, 1776. On the first of that month intelligence was received that a large British fleet was making its way towards Charleston, and on the morning of the fourth, the main part of this fleet came to anchor just outside of the bar. Preparations were immediately commenced to meet the expected attack.

About this time Maj. Gen. Charles Lee arrived in Charleston, and was invested by Gov. Rutledge with full command of all military affairs. He was disposed to withdraw all the troops from Sullivan's Island, but both Rutledge and Moultrie, who commanded the Island, dissuaded him from doing so. Fort Johnson, on the opposite side of the harbor, was occupied by the first South Carolina regular regiment, commanded by Col. Gadsden ; but it was their opinion that the chief defence of the city rested in Fort Sullivan, as it was then called. This stood on the front beach of Sullivan's Island, and commanded the main entrance to the harbor ; it was a square structure, with a bastion at each angle, and was built of Palmetto logs, piled one on another in two lines, sixteen feet apart, the space between being filled with sand. There was not sufficient time to carry out the plan of the fort, and only the wall on the front, and the south-eastern and part of the south-western sides were completed ; some temporary defences, built of plank, filled up the unfinished portions, but these were only available against a land attack. The armament consisted in all of twenty-six guns ; nine twenty-pounders, three eighteen-pounders, and fourteen twelve-pounders ; on the south-east bastion was the plain blue flag, with white crescent, which from that day became so famous.

At the eastern end of the Island breastworks were erected, and Col. William Thompson was in command. His whole force consisted of seven hundred and eighty men, and they were provided with one eighteen pounder and a field piece. The British land forces, three thousand men, under Maj. Gen. Clinton, landed on Long Island, and having fortified themselves there, began preparations to cross Beach Inlet and attack Fort Sullivan in the rear.

On the morning of the 28th of June, the fleet, under command of Admiral Sir Peter Parker, and consisting of eight vessels, two of them fifty gun ships, crossed the bar and advanced towards the city; at the same time Sir Henry Clinton's forces made a

Photo. by Barnard. FORT MOULTRIE. *Eng. by Photo. Eng. Co., N. Y.*

demonstration on the eastern end of the Island, but were kept in check by Col. Thompson's gallant riflemen.

Sir Peter Parker, supposing that the fort would

offer but a slight resistance, opened a brisk fire upon it as he passed, from four of his ships. The fire being as briskly returned, the engagement soon became general and lasted from a little before eleven in the forenoon to near nine o'clock at night, when the fleet retired, having suffered terrible losses; three of the vessels having been sent round to attack the fort on the western side, went aground on the shoal known as the middle ground, and one of them, the Actæon, could not be got off and was abandoned; the others escaped with severe losses; the Admiral's ship was almost entirely destroyed. The loss of the British was upwards of two hundred men; that of the Americans, was ten men killed and twenty-two wounded. The material of which the fort was composed favored the defenders; the spongy Palmetto logs did not splinter when struck, and, as later experience has proved, sand is far superior to masonry for resisting cannon shot. A morass in the interior of the fort did good service by putting out the fuses of many of the shells which fell into it.

One of the incidents of the day was the heroic rescue by Sergeant Jasper of the flag, which was shot away early in the action. He leapt over on the beach and deliberately restored it to its place, under the heaviest fire of the enemy.

The defence of this fort was one of the most gallant actions of the whole war, and gained for Gen. Moultrie the highest reputation. The fort was named, in honor of him, Fort Moultrie, which name it still bears. The present fort is built of brick, on the same site. It was occupied by United States troops, under Major Anderson, at the time of the secession of South Carolina, and it was his evacuation of it on the night of the 26th of December, 1860, after having spiked the guns and destroyed the carriages, and his taking possession of Fort Sumter, which constituted the first act of hostility in the war of secession.

When the Confederate troops occupied it they strengthened it with a glacis on the front, and with large bombproofs in the interior. It was garrisoned during the greater part of the war by the First Regular Infantry, Col. Butler, and took part in all the actions which occurred in Charleston harbor.

Since the war the United States authorities have removed the earthworks, and are now engaged in refitting and arming the fort.

The repulse of the British forces left Charleston in a state of comparative peace, the blockade being removed, commerce flourished, and notwithstanding the terrible fire of 15th January, 1778, in which two hundred and fifty dwellings, besides stores and other buildings, were destroyed, the city continued to grow and prosper until 1780, when the British recommenced military operations against it.

On the 11th February, 1780, a British army, under Sir Henry Clinton, landed within thirty miles of the city and commenced to advance upon it. Clinton formed a depot of supplies and built fortifications at Wappoo, on James' Island; on the first of April he crossed the Ashley and invested the city, at the same time his fleet crossed the bar, and this time passing

Fort Moultrie under a heavy fire, but without engaging it, sailed into the harbor.

The American forces of less than four thousand men, chiefly militia, under command of Gen. Lincoln, made active preparations for defence; strong lines of fortifications were thrown up across the Neck, and the works on South Bay, and other exposed parts of the city, strengthened and manned.

The British advanced by regular approaches, keeping up meantime a heavy bombardment; several skirmishes occurred between portions of the two armies, but there was no general engagement, and on the 12th of May, the enemy having carried the outer works, prepared for a general assault by land and sea, when the garrison, perceiving that further resistance was useless, and having already suffered heavily from sickness and want of food, determined to capitulate.

The British held the city until the 14th of December, 1782, and under their harsh rule the inhabitants had to endure many privations and indignities.

It was during this time that the execution of Col. Isaac Hayne took place. Col. Hayne was a planter of good family and high character. He had commanded a troop of horse during the war, but on the fall of Charleston, this was disbanded, and he retired with his family to his plantation; a short time afterwards, he was, on some pretence, induced to go to Charleston, where he was seized and imprisoned, until, in order to return to his dying wife, he consented, under protest, to take the oath of submission to the British authority; he had scarcely reached his home when a demand was made upon him to take up arms against his country. Conceiving that the contract had been violated, he made his escape and joined the American forces in the neighborhood. He was captured, and after a rigorous confinement for several months, in one of the rooms of the Exchange Building, on the 11th of August, 1781, he was taken thence to the place of execution, attended by an immense concourse of citizens, who had plead in vain for his release.

The indignation felt in the American army at this outrage was so great, that the officers addressed a memorial to Gen. Green, recommending immediate measures of retaliation, thereby exposing themselves to a similar fate in case of capture.

The occupation of the city by the British lasted, as we have said, until December, 1782. At that time the commander, General Leslie, having levelled the walls of the town and of Fort Johnson, notified Gen. Greene of the intended evacuation; and an arrangement was made for the American troops to enter the town as the British left it, both parties pledging themselves to abstain from any hostile demonstrations.

On the morning of the 14th of December the march commenced; the Americans following the British at a distance of two hundred yards, down the King street road until they were within the lines, when the British filed off to the left, to Gadsden's wharf, where they embarked in boats which were waiting to take them to the fleet. The following day the fleet left the harbor.

As may be supposed, great rejoicings followed this

event, and a new era of prosperity opened for the city. So far as Charleston was concerned, the war was virtually ended, and the general peace which was made soon after removed all further difficulties.

DESCRIPTION OF BUILDINGS, Etc.

With the return of peace the citizens of Charleston, under which name the city was incorporated 1783, were enabled to resume the exercise of that public spirit which they had previously displayed, and we find them soon establishing charitable institutions and erecting buildings to be permanent ornaments and improvements to the city.

And first and noblest among these institutions stands

THE CHARLESTON ORPHAN HOUSE.

The Act of Incorporation just referred to imposed upon the City the care of providing for the poor and maintaining and educating poor orphan children. In accordance with this Act, commissioners of the poor were appointed, and a number of orphan children were supported, by boarding them out in private houses, and were educated at the expense of the city.

In 1790, the City Council passed an Ordinance for the erection of an Orphan House, and the vacant lands between Boundary (now Calhoun) street and Vanderhorst street were appropriated to the purpose. On the 12th of November, 1792, the corner-stone of the building was laid by John Huger, Esq., Intendant of the City; and on the 18th of October, 1794, with appropriate religious services, one hundred and fifteen orphan children were introduced into it.

In 1853, the Commissioners presented a memorial to Council recommending the repair and enlargement of the building; and, this being adopted, Messrs. Jones & Lee, Architects, were charged with the work, which they completed shortly before the celebration of the sixty-sixth anniversary, October 18th, 1855.

The building as it now stands is in the Italian style; is two hundred and thirty-six feet long by seventy-six feet wide, with an extension in the rear ninety feet long by thirty-one feet wide. The main building is five stories high, divided in the front in three sections, the central portion being surmounted by a pediment and having an Italian portico projecting in front. The building is surmounted by a Mansard roof, and above the central section of the front is the belfry, in which is hung the city alarm bell; on the belfry is a figure of Charity. The whole height is one hundred and forty-six feet from the ground. It is divided into spacious and airy rooms, adapted to the various requirements of the inmates, and is surrounded by extensive grounds, well laid out, and protected by a high brick wall. In the northern part of the grounds is a handsome chapel, in which services are held every Sunday by some one of the city clergymen.

The institution is complete in every detail, and is Charleston's grandest work.

The lives of hundred of citizens, some of whom have risen to eminence in the nation, as well as in their own State, attest its practical value.

The statue of William Pitt, Earl of Chatham, which now stands in the Orphan House yard, is identified with the history of the city.

When the news of the repeal of the Stamp Act was received, May 3rd, 1766, the Commons House of Assembly, which was then in session, filled with enthusiastic gratitude to Mr. Pitt for his noble defence of their rights, unanimously resolved to procure a statue, to be erected in the province as a memorial of his great services. On the 31st of May, 1770, the statue, made in England, by Mr. Wilton, at a cost of £1,000 sterling, was landed in Charleston, and fixed upon a pedestal previously prepared for it, in the square at the intersection of Broad and Meeting streets, surrounded by an iron railing. During the siege of Charleston, a cannon ball from a British fort on James Island struck off the right arm, which was extended as if in the act of speaking; but it remained otherwise unhurt, until after the war it was found to interfere with travel through that thoroughfare, and was taken down and laid in the Orphan House yard. In 1808 the commissioners of the Orphan House obtained permission to erect it in its present place, in the centre of the enclosure, where it forms a conspicuous object.

The College of Charleston was incorporated in 1785, but nothing was done towards its establishment, except to collect some funds, until Dr. Smith offered to transfer the scholars of his academy to it. This offer was accepted, and a portion of the old brick barracks was fitted up, and possession taken in 1791; three years later the first commencement was held,

Photo. by Barnard. COLLEGE OF CHARLESTON. *Eng. by Photo. Eng. Co., N. Y.*

and six young men graduated, among them the late Bishop Bowen.

The college declined after this, however, and only a grammar school was maintained in the building for many years. At length an effort was made to reorganize and improve it, and this being liberally supported, a full collegiate course was adopted, with a grammar school attached, and the first commencement under the new organization was held in October, 1826. In 1837, an arrangement was made, by which the property of the college was transferred to the city, in trust for the re-establishment and maintenance of the institution on an improved plan. The college occupies the square bounded by George, Green, College, and St. Philip streets; it consists of a square, central building, fronting south on the campus, with extensive wings on the east and west; it is two stories, on a basement; the first story contains in the central building, the chapel, and in the wings, the recitation rooms; the second story is almost entirely occupied by the museum of natural history, a large and well arranged collection, gathered from all parts of the world, but specially interesting from the large number of specimens characteristic of South Carolina and the adjoining States.

The college library is in a small building of ornamental construction, in the western part of the campus. It has between five and six thousand volumes, of which two thousand were presented, in 1853, by Dr. L. A. Frampton, the present librarian; about twenty-five hundred more were bequeathed by the late Judge King.

MEDICAL COLLEGE OF THE STATE OF SOUTH CAROLINA.

This institution is located on the corner of Queen and Franklin streets, occupying a part of the square with the Roper Hospital, City Hospital, and County

Jail. It is one of the oldest medical schools at the South, and its very numerous alumni are scattered through the Southern States, many of them occupying the highest positions; some of them occupy

Photo. by Barnard. *Eng. by Photo. Eng. Co., N. Y.*

MEDICAL COLLEGE.

professorial chairs in the best Northern colleges; and some, like Drs. J. Marion Sims, and Prof. T. G. Thomas, of New York, have acquired a wide-spread reputation.

The charter of this College was obtained in 1832, but many of the original faculty, among whom we may mention Drs. S. H. Dickson and J. E. Holbrook, as specially distinguished, had been earlier engaged in teaching in another school, organized in 1822, by the Medical Society of South Carolina. This latter school was short lived, and, since its suspension, the present College has been the only regularly chartered Medical College in the State. Its career had been remarkably successful, until the late war so crippled the resources of the South as seriously to affect all institutions of learning. In common with the gradual improvement of the Southern country, the success of the College, under the new *regime*, is year by year becoming more assured. The present Faculty have done all in their power to meet the exigencies of the times, and to maintain the former prestige of the old institution. The fees for tuition have been made almost nominal, the idea being simply to pay the expenses of the school, without regard to the personal benefit to the teachers. This plan, which is considered only a temporary one, has been highly recommended by the Trustees and most of the old friends and Alumni of the College. We trust that students of medicine, at the South, will appreciate the efforts and liberal offers of the Faculty, and thus help to sustain a home institution which is so well endowed and ably conducted.

The following comprise the Board of Trustees and the Medical Faculty as now constituted:

Board of Trustees.—Hon. H. D. Lesesne, President; E. Horry Frost, Secretary and Treasurer; Hon. J. L. Manning, Hon. W. D. Porter, Gen. Wade Hampton, Hon. G. A. Trenholm, Hon. B. F. Perry, T. G. Prioleau, M. D., Henry Gourdin, Esq., Edward McCrady, Esq.

Medical Faculty.—R. A. Kinloch, M. D., Professor of the Principles and Practice of Surgery and Clinical Surgery: J. P. Chazal, M. D., Professor of Pathology and Practice of Medicine; Middleton Michel, M. D., Professor of Physiology; C. U. Shepard, Jr., M. D.. Professor of Chemistry; F. L. Parker, M. D., Professor of Anatomy; J. Ford Prioleau, M. D., Professor of Obstetrics and Gynæcology; F. Peyre Porcher, M. D., Professor of Materia Medica and Therapeutics, and of Clinical Medicine; Manning Simons, M. D., Demonstrator of Anatomy; Prof. R. A. Kinloch, Dean of the Faculty.

Connected with the Medical College, or rather more immediately with the Medical Society, is the Roper Hospital, which stands at the corner of Queen and Mazyck streets. This noble institution was founded through the liberality of Mr. Thomas Roper, whose name it bears. In 1854, he bequeathed real estate to the value of fifty thousand dollars for this purpose, the City of Charleston gave twenty thousand dollars, and the lot on which the Hospital stands; and in 1857 the State Legislature gave ten thousand dollars to complete the building, which was finished the following year. After the establishment of the Hospital, Mrs. Kohn also made a large bequest to it.

ROPER HOSPITAL.

The building is very handsome, and well arranged. The central portion has, on the first floor, offices for the physicians and others connected with the institution, on the second, the library of the Medical Society, and on the third, a large amphitheatre, provided for clinical lectures, for the medical students ; the east and west wings contain spacious and well ventilated wards, with broad piazzas to the south. In front is a tastefully laid out garden, which adds to the attractive appearance.

The Hospital was under control of the Medical Society, who appointed all the officers and superintended the conduct of the Institution, but in consequence of the losses sustained in the war, the funds are now put out at interest to accumulate, and the building is under lease to the city for ten years, as a general hospital.

In our early plan of Charles Town, we find in a conspicuous place the "Independent Church." This was established by Presbyterians, Congregationalists, and a few of the French Protestant Refugees. It afterwards became the Congregationalist Church. The original church was a small wooden building, which being remodelled, and enlarged, and painted white, was generally known as the "White Meeting House," and probably gave its name to Meeting street. On the same site the Circular Church, represented in our engraving, was built in 1804; it was curiously constructed, consisting of a rotunda eighty-eight feet in diameter, surmounted by a dome. On the western face was a square projection which supported the steeple, and, in front of this, a portico of six columns, surmounted by a pediment, formed the facade of the building. The cemetery extends back to that of St. Philip's Church. The church was destroyed by the fire of 1861, and only the picturesque ruins now occupy the site. The congregation have erected a small chapel, on the lot in which services are held.

Our illustration shows, adjoining the Circular Church, a building which was the scene of, perhaps, the most important event in the history of South Carolina; this was the Institute Hall, more lately known as Secession Hall. It was the property of the South Carolina Institute, an association for the promotion of the

CIRCULAR CHURCH AND INSTITUTE HALL.

industrial arts in the State, and was completed in 1854. The first floor was occupied by stores and offices, and the second contained an elegant and spacious hall, capable of holding twenty-five hundred persons; in it the annual Fairs of the Institute were held, and it was used for any specially large meetings. The National Democratic Convention, which met in Charleston, in April, 1860, held its meetings there; but the grand event which took place within its walls, was the ratification of the Ordinance of Secession. The State Convention held its meetings in St. Andrew's Hall, Broad street, until the adoption of the Ordinance of Secession, on the 20th of December, 1860, when it was resolved to adjourn to Institute Hall for the purpose of ratifying. At 6 P. M., on that day, the Convention moved in procession from St. Andrew's to the Institute Hall, where, after prayer by the Rev. John Bachman, D. D., the Ordinance was most solemnly ratified, receiving the signature of every member of the Convention. At the conclusion of the signing, the President of the Convention, Hon. D. F. Jamison, exhibited the parchment to the meeting, announcing that the Ordinance of Secession had been signed and ratified. He therefore proclaimed the State of South Carolina an Independent Commonwealth. On this announcement, the whole audience rose and gave vent to their enthusiasm by prolonged cheers, accompanied by the waving of hats and handkerchiefs. The occasion was celebrated in the evening by a general illumination and bonfires in the principal streets, and the parading of citizens with bands of music. This building, also, perished in the great fire, and its loss was deeply felt, as well for the associations connected with it, as for its intrinsic value.

The French Protestant Church belongs to the very

Photo. by Barnard. *Eng. by Photo. Eng. Co., N. Y.*

FRENCH PROTESTANT CHURCH.

early history of Charleston; the Huguenots, whose arrival in the province in 1685 and '86, we have already noticed, in a few years erected a building for worship on the site occupied by the present church, at the south-east corner of Church and Queen streets. The first building was destroyed by fire in 1740, a second met the same fate in 1796, and was rebuilt in 1797; about the year 1845, this was remodelled and enlarged to its present dimensions. It is still a small building, but a very pretty one, in correct Gothic style, carefully and neatly finished. On the walls of the interior are several handsome marble tablets, erected in memory of the principal founders of the church by their descendants.

It is worthy of remark that this is, probably, the only church in the United States which adheres to the exact form of the Huguenot worship.

In the year 1731, the strict Presbyterians, among the congregation of the Independent Church above described, left it, and established a church for themselves on the model of the Church of Scotland, and erected a building at the south-west corner of Meeting and Tradd streets. The present First Presbyterian or Scotch Church was built on the same site and was completed in 1814. It exhibits a fine front, composed of a recessed portico of four columns, flanked by two towers, surmounted by cupolas. The interior is spacious and well finished.

The Second Presbyterian Church, commonly known as Flinn's Church, from the name of its first pastor, Rev. Dr. Flinn, was built in 1811, the number of Presbyterians in the city having increased so much as to require more room. It stands at the corner of Charlotte and Elizabeth streets, on the highest spot in the city, and forms a very conspicuous landmark. It is of the temple form, and with its lofty portico, produces a fine effect. Behind this portico rises a tower, intended as the foundation of a steeple. The steeple has never been completed, but the height of the ground, as well as the great size of the Church itself, makes it visible at as great a distance as any of the other churches.

The cemetery surrounds the Church on three sides, the western front opening on a fine square, planted with grass and shade trees, and extending to Meeting street.

Photo. by Cook. *Eng. by Photo. Eng. Co., N. Y.*

SECOND PRESBYTERIAN, OR FLINN'S, CHURCH.

The Central (Third) Presbyterian Church stands on the western side of Meeting street, a short distance above Society street ; it is remarkable for the perfection of its architecture, having an elegant portico of pure Corinthian style, and the rest of the building

CENTRAL PRESBYTERIAN CHURCH.

corresponding in symmetry and correctness. It is without a steeple or other modern embellishment.

We have already alluded to the early establishment of the Baptists in Charleston. The site of their original building on the west side of Church street, a little above Water, is now occupied by the First Baptist Church, a building well worth notice, from its simple, but imposing architecture.

Photo. by Barnard. *Eng. by Photo. Eng. Co., N. Y.*

CITADEL SQUARE BAPTIST CHURCH.

The Citadel Square Baptist Church sprung from this. The idea of establishing it originated, in 1854, with Messrs. B. C. Pressley and C. L. Burckmeyer, who, after consultation with Rev. J. P. Boyce, formerly of the First Church, but then of Columbia, made known their design, and were promptly joined by a number of friends. A subscription was opened and was liberally filled up, more than one-half of the amount necessary for the building being subscribed by the heirs of the estate of Mr. Ker Boyce. A lot was procured at the corner of Meeting and Henrietta streets, and work commenced on the building, which was rapidly completed, and was dedicated on the 23d of November, 1856.

The members of the Wentworth street church soon after joined themselves to the congregation.

Photo. by Barnard. BETHEL CHURCH. *Eng. by Photo. Eng. Co., N. Y.*

The style of the building is Norman. Its extreme dimensions are eighty feet on Meeting street, and one hundred and forty-five feet on Henrietta street; the side walls are forty feet high, and the west or front wall seventy feet to the point of the gable. The interior will accommodate one thousand persons. The tower is located at the north-west corner of the main building. It is square, supported by buttresses at the angles, and, with the spire, is two

Photo. by Barnard. *Eng. by Photo. Eng. Co., N. Y.*

ST. JOHN'S CHAPEL.

hundred and twenty feet high. The whole building presents an elegant and impressive appearance.

The Methodist Church was organized in America in 1784; the denomination flourished in Charleston, and now has several churches, with large congregations, in the city. Bethel Church, the Second Metho dist, is situated on the south side of Calhoun street, near Pitt. It is a large brick building, roughcast, with a fine portico in front, and surrounded by an extensive yard. It is one of the largest and best attended Methodist Churches in Charleston. The old wooden church that preceded the present building, and was erected about 1800, has been removed to the rear, and is occupied by a numerous colored congregation.

St. John's Chapel (Episcopal), at the corner of Amherst and Hanover streets, affords a convenient place of worship for the Episcopalians residing in the north-eastern portion of the city.

St. Mary's Church, situated on the south side of Hasel street, between King and Meeting streets, was the first Roman Catholic church in Charleston, and, since the burning of St. Finbar's, is the largest; it is an unpretending building, but is neatly finished inside, and the altar is richly decorated.

ST. FINBAR'S CATHEDRAL.

The ruins of this beautiful building stand on a lot which was once the old Vaux-Hall Garden, at the north-east corner of Broad and Friend streets. The cathedral was built on the site of the old St. Finbar's, a wooden building; the corner-stone was laid in 1852, and it was dedicated in April, 1854. It was of brown freestone and was the most beautiful church edifice in the city. The height to the top of the cross was two hundred and eighteen and a half feet; the exterior dimensions were, from front to rear of vestry, one hundred and ninety-four feet: height to roof ridge of the rear, seventy-seven feet; width, seventy-three feet. The building cost, when completed, $106,000,

Photo. by Barnard. *Eng. by Photo. Eng. Co., N. Y.*

ST. MARY'S [CATHOLIC] CHURCH.

and was complete in every respect; the interior was very highly ornamented, the windows all of stained glass, and the decorations of the altar elaborate and tasteful. It was destroyed by the fire of December, 1861. A few years later, when time had somewhat softened the effects of the fire, its ruins presented a most beautiful picture. A considerable part of the graceful steeple remained, but this was thought to be dangerous, and most of it was taken down.

Photo. by Barnard. *Eng. by Photo. Eng. Co., N. Y.*

HEBREW CHURCH.

The Unitarian Church was originally an offshoot of the old Independent Church, and remained connected with it until the year 1817. The congregation adopted the Unitarian doctrines about the year 1819. The first building on the site of the present one, on the east side of Archdale street, a short way above Queen street, was begun just before the revolution, and was finished shortly after that war.

The new building was erected on the foundation of the old one, and was dedicated on the 2d of April, 1854, It is the most perfect piece of architecture of its kind, in the city. The style is the "Perpendicular," the latest and richest of all the styles of Gothic architecture. Every part of the building, exterior and interior, is complete; the ceiling of the nave is that peculiar Gothic work, styled "fan tracery," and is exquisitely rich and beautiful. The great window in the rear of the church is in the richest style of design and finish, and is filled with figures of emblematic character.

St. John's Lutheran Church, which stands immediately north of this, is in marked contrast, being of perfectly simple design.

A Hebrew congregation existed in Charleston as early as 1750; in 1795 they purchased the site of their present synagogue on the north side of Hasel street, between King and Meeting streets. The synagogue is a brown stone building, in the Athenian style, very handsomely built, but lacking the proper situation to show it off to advantage.

HISTORY OF CHARLESTON.

[CONTINUED.]

We turn from the description of the buildings which illustrate the growth and progress of the city, to notice certain events which exhibited the characteristics of the people and affected their action on subsequent occasions.

The Mexican war afforded an opportunity for the military spirit of the younger portion of the community of Charleston, and of the rest of the State, to manifest itself. On its breaking out, in 1847, the famous Palmetto Regiment was organized. This splendid body of men was composed of the very best material of the State, and Charleston was largely represented in it. The regiment was in nearly every action of the war, and distinguished itself always; whether in battle or in severe marches and arduous duties, it was second to none in courage and endurance. It was the flag of the Palmetto Regiment that was first planted on the walls of the conquered city of Mexico. But it paid the penalty of its galantry by terrible losses. Colonel Butler, the commander, was killed while heading a charge; Lieutenant-Colonel Dickinson, who succeeded to the command, perished in like manner; scarcely three hundred men out of near twelve hundred returned to Carolina. They were received with enthusiasm everywhere, and the State awarded a medal to each of them. A very beautiful monument was erected to the dead, consisting of a perfect representation of a Palmetto tree in iron, upon a pedestal, on which were engraved in letters of brass the names of those who had fallen. This was intended to be placed in the new State House at Columbia.

Many of the survivors of the Palmetto Regiment were in the field, in the war of secession, and added to the laurels they had already gained; several rose to distinguished positions.

For many years after the Revolution, Charleston continued in a profoundly peaceful condition; the war with Great Britain of 1812, did not seriously affect her; naturally there were occasional stoppages of trade, and threats of attack, but nothing came of these beyond exciting in the people that prompt spirit of resistance to force, which they have always exhibited.

This happy condition of affairs continued unbroken until the celebrated Nullification excitement, which threatened the country at large, with the contest which actually occurred in 1860, and in South Carolina, particularly in Charleston, caused the formation of parties which remained in opposition up to that time. The various questions involved in this matter cannot be treated in our space; the main issue was upon the right of a State to *nullify*, to declare unconstitutional and void, an Act of Congress.

South Carolina took the lead in this, as she has done on many occasions, in the history of the country. Mr. Calhoun was the great leader, along with

Gen. Robt. Y. Hayne, and other eminent men, while the opposition numbered in its ranks such men as Mr. Legare, Judge Huger, Mr. Petigru, and others. A contest in regard to such grave matters, and with such men arrayed on each side, could not fail to awaken the interest and enthusiasm of every citizen.

The tariff laws proposed in Congress were, in the opinion of many Southern statesmen, directly inimical to the interests of the Southern States. For several years the question was agitated. In 1827, Mr. Calhoun published his views. On the fourth of July, 1831, addresses were made by the leaders of each side, which drew the party lines distinctly, and on the 23d of November, 1832, the General Assembly called a Convention. This Convention, with Governor Hamilton at its head, by a very large majority, passed the Nullification Ordinance, ignoring certain acts of Congress.

On the 10th of December, the President of the United States, Andrew Jackson, published a proclamation denouncing the Ordinance. Thus the State and the United States Government were openly at issue, and, as may readily be imagined, the feelings of all parties were wrought up to the highest pitch. Mr. Clay's compromise bill, however, introduced the following February, and the arrival of a commissioner from Virginia to promote an adjustment, tended to allay the excitement, and on the 15th of March, 1833, the Nullification Ordinance was revoked and quiet restored. But at no period in the history of the State have politics assumed such a violent and personal aspect as at this. The community was divided against itself, and it seemed scarcely possible to avert a violent contest among its members.

The secession movement involved far more important issues, and the enthusiasm was greater and more general; but, although at that time there was some eminent men who were opposed to secession, the majority in favor of it was so overwhelmingly large, that their opposition never took shape, and in fact, they generally yielded to the manifest spirit of the people and cast in their lot with them; hence, the action of the State might justly be called unanimous. On the question of Nullification, views were divided, and it was not uncommon for members of the same household to be directly opposed to each other. On the 31st of March, 1850, South Carolina was called to mourn the loss of her greatest statesman, Hon. John C. Calhoun, who died in the very midst of this work, as Senator in Washington.

He was buried, as we have already mentioned, in the cemetery of St. Philip's Church, and his funeral was the most impressive sight of its kind ever witnessed in Charleston. On the 26th of April, the remains, enclosed in an iron coffin, reached Charleston in charge of committees of the United States Senate and House of Representatives, and of several of the States; they were taken in a magnificent funeral car, with a large escort, to the citadel, the entire front of which was draped in mourning; there they were received from the Senate committee by Hon. T. Leger Hutchinson, Mayor of the city. A procession was then formed, comprising every military and civic organization in the city, besides the seamen, children of the schools, and hundreds of citizens of this and the adjoining States, on foot and on horseback, and

Photo. by Barnard. *Eng. by Photo. Eng. Co., N. Y.*

THE CITY HALL.

moved through the principal streets to the City Hall, where the remains were placed in a splendid catafalque, prepared for their reception. Here the body lay in state until the next day, under the special charge of an honorary guard of two hundred citizens. During the day thousands of citizens and strangers repaired to the City Hall, to pay their tribute of respect to the illustrious dead. The most perfect order and decorum prevailed; the stream of visitors entered the main doors, ascended the catafalque, and after gazing silently on the sarcophagus, retired through the passage in the rear.

The coffin and sarcophagus enclosing it were covered with flowers, the offerings of the ladies of the city.

The next day the body was removed, with a civic procession, to St. Philip's Church, where the burial services were read by the Right Rev. Dr. Gadsden, Bishop of the Diocese, and a funeral discourse preached by the Rev. James W. Miles. It was then borne to the western cemetery, and there placed in the vault prepared for its temporary reception.

The whole of the ceremonies were conducted in the most solemn and impressive manner, and no effort was spared by the citizens to mark their sense of respect for the deceased and their grief for his loss.

The action of the people of Charleston and of the State generally on this occasion was significant. It was no mere outburst of sentiment. It arose not only from the great love and reverence which Mr. Calhoun's purity of character and intellect inspired, and the pride which they felt in him as one of the greatest statesmen that America has produced, but it was also occasioned by the intense sympathy with and belief in the political principles which he represented. The States Rights doctrines which he believed in and taught were thoroughly impressed upon their minds, and undoubtedly influenced the whole future conduct of the State.

The extensive square of the Citadel Green, overlooked by the castellated buildings at the Academy, affords one of the most pleasing sights in Charleston, and is connected, by many associations, with her palmiest days. It was the rendezvous on all occa-

Photo. by Barnard. THE CITADEL. *Eng. by Photo. Eng. Co., N. Y.*

sions when military or civic parades took place, and many brilliant processions made it their starting point.

The Academy was an object of great interest to the people of Charleston. In 1842 the Legislature transferred the appropriation for the Citadel and Magazine Guard at Charleston, and the Arsenal Guard, at Columbia, to a board of visitors, who were authorized to organize the State Military Academy.

In February, 1843, this organization was effected, and the cadets required to discharge the duties of a State Guard. This building had been the Arsenal, and was occupied, until about 1832, by United States troops, and then by regular State troops, until the formation of the Academy. It was of two stories, without the wings, the third story was added, and the wings constructed to extend the Arsenal.

The Academy was admirably conducted, the drill and discipline of the cadets were unsurpassed, and the tone of the institution very high. To it the State owes many of her best men in all the walks of life.

On the breaking out of the late war the Cadets were early in the field. In fact, the first gun of the conflict was fired by them, on the memorable morning of the 9th of January, 1861, when the Star of the West attempted to re-inforce Fort Sumter; after that they were kept at their studies in the Academy, and doing guard duty in and around the city, and whenever an emergency arose, they were promptly out and did good service. About December, 1864, they went into active service, and so remained until the close of the war, the Academy being virtually abandoned. On the evacuation of Charleston, the United States troops took possession of the buildings and the larger part of the garrison is still quartered in them. It is much to be regretted that the property is not returned to the State and the Academy revived.

The Market Hall fronts on Meeting street. It is a fine building, in temple form, standing on a high open basement, having a lofty portico in front, reached by a double flight of stone steps, the exterior cornices are appropriately ornamented with bulls' heads.

In rear of this building are the markets, consisting of a row of low sheds, supported by brick arches,

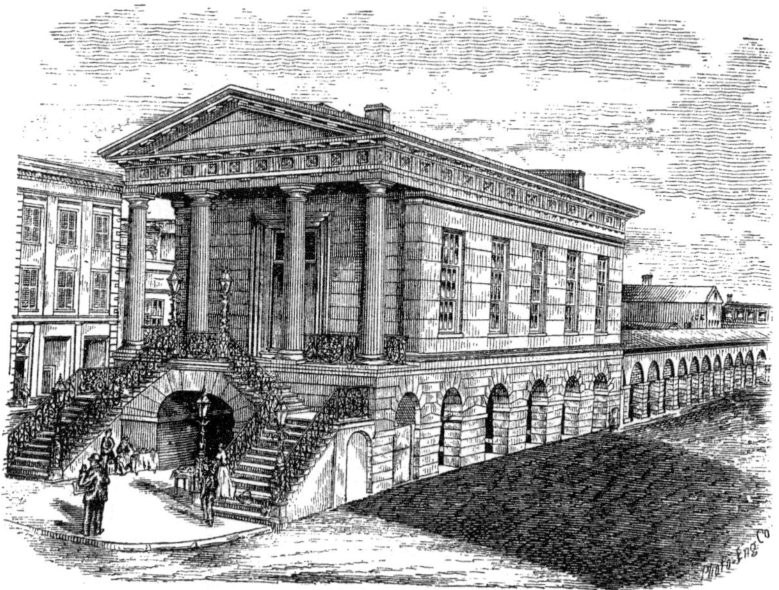

Photo. by Barnard. MARKET HALL. *Eng. by Photo. Eng. Co., N. Y.*

and extending to East Bay street. They have divisions for large and small meats, vegetables and fish, the stalls being arranged on each side, having a broad, shady walk between them. The whole arrangement is a judicious and convenient one, especially for a Southern climate.

The Hibernian Hall, on the west side of Meeting street, a short distance above Broad, is the property of the Hibernian Society, one of the oldest and wealthiest associations in the city, and comprising in its ranks all of the best citizens of Irish extraction.

Photo. by Barnard. *Eng. by Photo. Eng. Co., N. Y.*

HIBERNIAN HALL.

The building is a handsome and substantial one, conveniently arranged, with a large hall, occupying the whole of the second floor, and a smaller hall, and committee rooms below. Since the burning of the

Institute and St. Andrew's Halls, this one has been used for all large assemblies; it was also arranged for a theatre, and used by all theatrical performances until the building of the Academy of Music. The society have lately put it in thorough repair, and ornamented it quite handsomely.

The new Custom House, an engraving of which appears on page 6, which is only partially completed, presents, even in that condition, one of the handsomest objects in Charleston.

It is situated just south of the Market wharf, on Cooper River; the site, which was formerly known as Fitzsimmons' wharf, was purchased by the United States Government in 1849, and, in 1850, Col. E. B. White received the appointment as superintendent, and the work was commenced and continued until the war arrested its progress. It is on a grand scale; the foundation consists of seven thousand thirty-feet piles, on which rests a heavy layer of grillage, then follows a thickness of eighteen inches of concrete, on which stand a number of inverted arches, built of brick, and about ten feet in height; the superstructure rises from these These details will serve to give some idea of the magnitude of the work proposed. It has already cost some hundreds of thousands of dollars, and it will take many thousands more to complete it. Since the war, appropriations have been made from time to time for the continuation of the work, but no steady progress has been made. The building is of white marble; the style of architecture the Roman-Corinthian; some changes have been made in the original plans which are not yet fully carried out, and prevent further description at this time.

We come now to the period in the history of Charleston which overshadows all the rest in importance, both in the material changes which it produced

Photo. by Barnard. *Eng. by Photo. Eng. Co., N. Y.*

EAST BATTERY.

in the city itself and in the qualities and characteristics of its citizens which it brought into play.

Charleston, as she had done in the throwing off the government of the Lords Proprietors in 1719, in the Revolution of 1776, and in the Nullification proceedings of 1831, took the lead among the cities of the South in the Secession movement of 1860–61; we have already described the scenes which took place in the Institute Hall, on the evening of the 20th of December, 1860. The people of Charleston were ready to abide by any consequences that might result from their action on that occasion, but they hoped that the United States Government would recognize their rights and not resort to forcible means of settling the questions between the Southern States and itself. This hope was first shaken when, on the night of the 26th of December, Major Anderson, Commandant of Fort Moultrie, abandoned that fort, having first spiked the guns and destroyed the carriages, and took possession of Fort Sumter. By this action war was virtually declared, and the State authorities deemed it advisable to look to their own defences; accordingly the following day Castle Pinckney and Fort Moultrie were occupied by volunteer commands—Castle Pinckney by the Rifle Battalion, Col. J. Johnston Pettigrew, Fort Moultrie, by four companies of artillery, under Col. W. G. DeSaussure.

Other points around the harbor were fortified and manned by companies from the city, and other parts of the State. A detachment of the Citadel Cadets, under Major P. F. Stevens, occupied a battery, hastily thrown up on the point of Morris Island. On the morning of the 9th of January, 1861, the Star of the West, a United States transport steamer, loaded with men and military stores, attempted to enter the harbor for the purpose of reinforcing Fort Sumter. When about two miles from the fort, the cadets opened fire upon her; the first shot was fired across her bow, merely to give warning. The steamer running up the United States flag, and increasing her speed, the next shots were aimed at her, and one struck, while the rest were so close as to show that the artillerists had got the range and were ready to do damage. Perceiving that, the Captain deemed it more prudent to retreat, and turned his vessel seaward, abandoning the project of aiding the fort.

Thus the cadets had the honor of firing the first gun of the war, and the prestige which they acquired on this occasion never left them. Whenever called into the field they were placed in the position of danger and of honor.

From this time all doubts were removed from the minds of the people of South Carolina as to the hostile intentions of the United States Government.

Gen. G. T. Beauregard having arrived in Charleston, from New Orleans, was invested by Gov. Pickens with command of all military affairs, and proceeded at once to organize his forces.

It was evident that the garrison of Fort Sumter could not remain there with safety to the city, but Major Anderson showed no signs of intention to move, and it was ascertained that ships of war were on their way to the South; a special messenger, also, from President Lincoln, informed Governor Pickens and General Beauregard that the fort was to be provisioned by force. Preparations must, therefore, be made on our side to anticipate this. Batteries were thrown up on Morris and Sullivan's Islands, Fort

Moultrie was strengthened, and a floating battery, protected with iron sheathing, was built and anchored off Haddrell's Point.

Volunteer companies were raised throughout the State, and equipped and drilled as thoroughly as time and means would allow, and every preparation

Photo. by Barnard. *Eng. by Photo. Eng. Co., N. Y.*

FORT SUMTER.

possible, under the circumstances, was made for a resort to arms if it should prove necessary. By this time several of the other Southern States had followed the lead of South Carolina, and the Confederate Government was, to some extent, at least, organized; Gen. Beauregard, therefore, acted under the orders of the Secretary of War, Hon. L. P. Walker, whose instructions were not to permit troops or provisions to be thrown into Fort Sumter, and to use such means as he should deem proper to prevent such an attempt.

At twelve o'clock, on the 11th of April, Gen. Beauregard made a formal demand for the surrender of the Fort. Major Anderson replied: "I have the honor to acknowledge the receipt of your communication, demanding the evacuation of this fort, and to say in reply thereto, that it is a demand with which I regret that my sense of honor and my obligations to my government prevent my compliance." He added, "Probably I will await the first shot, and if you do not batter us to pieces, we will be starved out in a few days."

On the same day Gen. Beauregard received a despatch from the Secretary of War, authorizing him to propose that if Maj. Anderson would name a time at which he would evacuate the fort, and would not in the mean time use his guns against the Confederate forces, no attack should be made upon the fort, and thus, bloodshed might be avoided. Maj. Anderson refusing to accept these terms, Gen. Beauregard proceeded to action.

At twenty minutes past four o'clock, on Friday morning, April 12th, Fort Moultrie opened fire.

The effect of the sound of these guns in the city was electrical. In a moment, almost, the streets were

Photo. by Barnard. SOUTH BATTERY. *Eng. by Photo. Eng. Co., N. Y.*

thronged with people hastening to every point which commanded a view of the harbor, where they remained hour after hour, watching with breathless anxiety the result of the encounter.

Fort Sumter replied to the guns of Moultrie with three barbette guns, and then the batteries on Cummings Point, Mount Pleasant, Fort Johnson, and the Floating Battery, commenced a rapid bombardment.

Between seven and eight o'clock, Major Anderson brought into play the two tiers of guns looking towards Fort Moultrie and the Stevens' Iron Battery on Cummings Point, and then the firing from Sumter became rapid; it was directed chiefly against those batteries and the Floating Battery anchored off Haddrell's Point. Five of the Confederate batteries kept up the fire; the rest were held in reserve in case of an attempt on the part of the fleet to enter the harbor.

With the exception of an interruption of about three hours, caused by a heavy rain storm, the bombardment continued unceasingly through the whole day and night; during the night Fort Sumter was silent, the garrison being employed in repairing damages, and adding some protections to the barbette guns. At seven next morning, Major Anderson opened a heavy and rapid fire, which was kept up for two hours steadily. In the meantime the red hot shot which was thrown from Fort Moultrie had ignited the officer's quarters in Sumter, which were of wood, and a terrible fire was raging within the fort. Every effort was made by the garrison to conquer it, but without success, and it soon became evident that the fort could no longer be held. The flag was by this time shot away and was replaced by a flag of truce. When the fire was perceived to be raging, Colonel Wigfall, of General Beauregard's staff, went to the fort, under a flag of truce, to offer assistance in putting it out; he informed Major Anderson that the firing from our batteries would cease as soon as the United States flag was hauled down, which was accordingly done, the only time, be it remembered, that the flag of Sumter was ever lowered in the presence of an enemy.

The same flag was, in 1865, again raised on the ramparts, with considerable ceremony, but the performance was somewhat lacking in glory, for the Confederates had evacuated the fort many hours before, and were miles away out of sight and hearing.

When the flag was hauled down, Senator Chesnut and ex-Governor Manning went to the fort, and stipulated with Major Anderson that his surrender should be unconditional, subject to such terms as Gen. Beauregard should dictate. These were very generous. Gen. Beauregard refused to receive Major Anderson's sword, and complimented him and his officers on their gallant defence. The garrison were permitted to take with them all their arms and personal effects. They left on Monday morning, in the steamer Baltic, for New York.

Thus ended the first battle of the war. The bombardment lasted forty hours, and upwards of three thousand shot and shell were fired, most of them aimed with precision, but the strangest fact in regard to it is, that not a life was lost on either side. The first victory of the Confederates was entirely bloodless.

For several months military preparations had been going on vigorously in the city, and the fall of Sumter only quickened these, for it was evident that the United States Government was determined on war. Those were stirring times in Charleston. Volunteer commands were organized, which included the citizens of every class, condition, and age, and which were diligently drilled and exercised. The streets were alive at all hours of the day, with men in uniform hurrying to the different places of rendezvous, and the public squares were the constant scenes of military manœuvres of every description. Great

Photo. by Barnard. *Eng. by Photo. Eng. Co., N. Y.*

POST OFFICE FRONT VIEW.

liberality was displayed by the citizens at this time; money was freely subscribed for every purpose for which it might be needed, and in many instances wealthy men armed and equipped entire companies at their own expense.

Although the serious nature of the affairs they were embarked upon was not forgotten by the Charlestonians, yet the season was one almost of gayety. The call for active preparations stimulated the spirits and energies of all. The ladies were as enthusiastic as the men, and did everything in their power to aid and encourage the defenders of the cause they held dear. Very early in the war the women of the South commenced that course of self-denial among themselves, and active assistance, as well as comfort and encouragement, to the men, which characterized their conduct throughout the whole struggle, and more especially in the miseries of the terrible peace which followed it. Soon the notes of war sounded from Virginia, and all the troops which could be spared from the defences of the State promptly offered themselves; and then commenced those partings which each year brought greater sadness to the homes of the South.

As we have said, the preparations for the defence of Charleston were actively carried on; Fort Sumter and the batteries around the harbor were strengthened and heavily armed; fortifications were built at every point where they could be made available against the enemy's fleet, and equal provision was made against attack by land. Across the Neck a complete line of entrenchments was thrown up, and even in the city itself batteries were erected on such points as commanded the harbor, or the land approach. But for some time no demonstrations were made, sufficiently important to need mention in this brief sketch. The fleet blockaded the harbor, and occasionally made a feint of attempting to enter it, but the commanders perceived that the defences were too strong for them, and contented themselves with endeavoring to cut off supplies from abroad by the destruction of such of the blockade-runners as they could catch, not a very successful business, however, for numbers of swift vessels, manned by skillful and courageous sailors, passed under the very guns of the largest war vessels, and landed their cargoes at the wharves of the city.

Meanwhile a peculiar calm brooded over the city. The first hurry and excitement was over and the war had become a reality. Those of the citizens who were not called into active service, pursued, as far as might be, their usual avocations, but it was with the quiet and gravity of men who awaited the issue of great events.

The city, as she then stood, is described in perfect verse by Carolina's truest poet :

" Calm as that second summer which precedes
The first fall of the snow,
In the broad sunlight of heroic deeds,
The city hides the foe.

" As yet behind their ramparts, stern and proud,
Her bolted thunders sleep—
Dark Sumter, like a battlemented cloud,
Looms o'er the solemn deep.

" No Calpe frowns from lofty cliff or scar
To guard the holy strand ;
But Moultrie holds in leash her dogs of war
Above the level sand.

"And down the dunes a thousand guns lie couched,
Unseen, beside the flood—
Like tigers in some Orient jungle crouched,
That wait and watch for blood.

"Meanwhile, through streets still echoing with trade,
Walk grave and thoughtful men,
Whose hands may one day wield the patriot's blade
As lightly as the pen.

"And maidens with such eyes as would grow dim
Over a bleeding hound,
Seem each one to have caught the strength of him
Whose sword she sadly bound.

"Thus girt without and garrisoned at home,
Day patient following day,
Old Charleston looks from roof, and spire, and dome,
Across her tranquil bay.

* * * * * * * * *

"Shall the spring dawn, and she still clad in smiles,
And with an unscathed brow,
Rest in the strong arms of her palm-crowned isles,
As fair and free as now?

"We know not; in the temple of the Fates
God has inscribed her doom;
And, all untroubled in her faith, she waits
The triumph or the tomb."

But as time went on, the engagements which were taking place at points more or less near the city, were warning the inhabitants that their time of trial was approaching, and calling more and more of the men to the outworks, while the non-combatants were seeking securer places in the interior of the State. Space only permits the mention of a few of these actions, which were in the immediate neighborhood of the city.

The battle of Secessionville, James Island, on the

16th June, 1862, was one of the most important. Secessionville was occupied by a regiment of artillery under Col. Lamar, and its fortifications were only in progress, and far from complete, when the attack was made. The Charleston Battalion, Col. P. C. Gaillard, the Eutaw Regiment, Col. C. H. Simonton, and the Louisiana Battalion, Major Hutson, were engaged along with Col. Lamar's Artillery. The enemy, in large force, charged the works in front three times without success, and then attempted to take them by a flank movement, which was also repulsed. The battle which was closely contested for several hours, and was splendidly fought, resulted in the victory of the Confederates, who lost fifty-three killed, and one hundred and thirty-four wounded; the loss of the enemy was heavy, amounting to upwards of five hundred. Among the killed on our side were several prominent Charlestonians, whose loss was deeply felt.

On Saturday, the 31st January, 1863, the Confederate iron-clad gunboats, Palmetto State, Capt. John Rutledge, and Chicora, Capt. John R. Tucker, made a descent upon the blockading fleet at the mouth of the harbor. The expedition was under command of Commodore D. N. Ingraham, who was on board the Palmetto State; they came upon the blockaders under cover of a haze, and the Palmetto State struck the Mercedita, a sloop of war, before she was perceived by those on board, and left her in a sinking condition; the crew having surrendered, were parolled. The Chicora opened fire at short range on several large steamers. The fleet was completely taken by surprise, and promptly dispersed and disappeared, though only for a short time.

On Tuesday, April 8th, of the same year, an attack was made by the enemy's fleet on Fort Sumter ; they advanced in two lines of battle; as they neared the fort, Col. Rhett, the commandant, had the long roll beaten, and the garrison, regimental, and Palmetto flags run up and saluted. Fort Moultrie commenced firing, and was followed immediately by Fort Sumter, and the batteries on Sullivans' and Morris' Islands. The Passaic, the leading vessel of the first line, took position about fourteen hundred yards from the fort ; after being under fire for about thirty minutes, and having been several times struck, she drew out of range, and her place was taken for about the same length of time, by each of the other vessels of that line. Then came the Ironsides, an immense frigate, with an armament of fourteen eleven-inch guns, and two two-hundred pound rifled guns ; but her great size made her too good a target, and she was compelled to retire.

The second line then advanced, the Keokuk, a double-turretted monitor leading ; a terrific fire was poured upon her, which she stood for about half an hour, and then withdrew, so badly damaged that she sunk at her moorings the next morning. About ninety shots were fired by the fleet, forty of which struck Fort Sumter ; there were no casualties, but the fort sustained considerable injury.

On Friday, July 10th, at half past five in the morning, the enemy opened fire from batteries on Folly

Island, on the works on the extreme south end of Morris Island, commanded by Capt. J. C. Mitchell; after a severe bombardment, to which Capt. Mitchell could only reply slowly, and without much effect, his guns being small and few in number, a large force was landed, which was at once attacked by Capt. Mitchell, now reinforced by Col. Graham's regiment of infantry, but the Confederates were outnumbered, and were compelled to fall back towards Battery Wagner, the principal defence of the island; the enemy advancing and forming in line of battle was again attacked by the Confederates, further reinforced, but still greatly inferior in numbers; but after a fierce encounter, they were compelled to retreat into the fort. Four determined efforts were made to take it by storm, but were repulsed. Then commenced the siege of Battery Wagner, the defence of which stands second only to that of Fort Sumter, in the courage with which it was maintained, and the terrible hardships the defenders had to undergo.

On the night of the 14th, Col. Rion, with between two and three hundred men, made a successful sortie on the enemies lines, but their force was too large to be dislodged by such means.

A furious bombardment was kept up daily on the fort. On the 18th, this was maintained steadily for eleven hours, from sixty-five heavy guns and eight mortars; the shot and shell fell upon the fort at the rate of twenty-seven a minute. At eight o'clock, in the evening, the enemy advanced in two columns, of three thousand each, under command of Brigadier-

General Strong, and a desperate assault was made upon the fort. A hand-to-hand fight ensued, which lasted for three hours, and resulted in the complete defeat of the attacking party, with six hundred men left on the field, and a total loss of above fifteen hundred. Our loss was about one hundred.

The siege of Battery Wagner lasted forty-eight days, and, as we have said, was marked with the most splendid courage. A fire was kept up, which never ceased except for the purpose of an assault, and the besieged were subjected to almost unparalleled hardships. The confinement to close bombproofs, often half filled with dead and dying men, the difficulty of obtaining water or cooked food, besides the continual labors of the defence, made it almost impossible for any constitution to stand more than two or three days at a time, and yet it was frequently necessary to wait many hours for a boat to escape the guns of the enemy and land the relief.

At length it was perceived that Morris' Island could no longer be held; and, accordingly, on the night of the 6th of September, Batteries Wagner and Gregg were quietly evacuated. They had been mined and the slow-match was lighted at Battery Wagner, by Capt. Huguenin, and at Battery Gregg, by Capt. Lesesne, but, owing to defective fuses, the magazines did not explode.

On Friday night, August the 21st, 1863, a communication was received at General Beauregard's headquarters from Gen. Gilmore, the United States Commander on Morris' Island, demanding the evacuation of that Island and Fort Sumter, and stating that if the demand was not complied with in four hours from the time of the delivery of his note at Fort Wagner, he would open fire on the city. This communication was without signature. Gen. Beauregard being absent on a reconnoisance, it was received by Gen. Jordan, his Chief of Staff, who returned it to be signed. It was signed and received again at nine o'clock next morning. In the mean time the threat was carried out; between one and two o'clock, on Saturday morning, the firing commenced, and thirteen shells were thrown into the city, at intervals of fifteen minutes; the bursting of the gun put a stop to it after that number. No damage was done, but, naturally, it was the cause of considerable excitement and alarm. Gen. Beauregard wrote a letter of indignant remonstrance to Gen. Gilmore for having fired on the city without notice, and without opportunity having been given for the removal of the women and children..

The bombardment commenced on this occasion was kept up, with scarcely an intermission, until the evacuation of the city, on the 18th of February, 1865, a period of five hundred and eighty-six days. Of course, considerable damage was done to property in the city; but the casualties were very few, and it was astonishing to observe how soon the people became used to it and went about their daily avocations. It soon became necessary to withdraw from the more exposed positions; and on the 25th of August the Post Office was removed to the corner of King and

Ann streets. By degrees other public offices were removed to the upper part of the city, and most persons took up their residence there, but it was all done quietly and without any panic or even excitement.

From this time on little remains to be told of Charleston in the war. The shelling continued from day to day, with more or less violence, and by degrees the inhabited space was contracted, and more and more of the non-combatants were removed to what seemed safer places, but there was no thought of giving up the city, until Sherman had reached the sea, and was marching up from the South; then it became evident that Charleston must be abandoned. The evacuation commenced on the evening of the 17th of February, 1865, and, by the morning of the 18th, the troops had been quietly withdrawn from the batteries around the harbor and from the city itself, which was left in charge of the Mayor, Hon. Charles Macbeth, who remained to preserve order and prevent destruction as far as possible. About ten o'clock, the Mayor communicated with the United States officers, who were seen approaching the city, informing them that the military had left it. The United States authorities then took possession. The city was at this time in considerable danger of total destruction. The Confederates, before leaving, had collected all the cotton in the various stores and warehouses into piles, and set fire to it; this was hastily and, in some cases, carelessly done, and the result was that many of the buildings in the neighborhood of these piles of cotton took fire; most of them were, with some difficulty, put out; but in one instance the destruction both of life and property was terrible. At the Northeastern Railroad depot a large quantity of provisions was left, around which a crowd of the poor people of the neighborhood had eagerly gathered; along with the provisions was stored a considerable amount of cannon-powder, made up into cartridges, and some boys were amusing themselves by throwing handfuls of this powder on a fire which was burning in the yard; by some means a spark reached the pile of cartridges, and a terrific explosion occurred, which, in an instant, demolished the whole building, leaving a fierce fire burning among its ruins. This spread rapidly, and resulted in the almost entire destruction of two squares. What was the number of lives lost has never been ascertained, but it is estimated at certainly not less than one hundred.

This, and the other fires, caused in the course of that one morning the loss of thousands of dollars worth of property.

The city was now left in the hands of the enemy, who had so long been vainly endeavoring to seize it; and while the oft repeated threats of razing it to the ground were not literally carried out, yet quite sufficient damage was done to satisfy the most revengeful spirit. Private houses, as well as public buildings, were turned over to the military, and, worse still, to their followers; and, for some weeks at least, a continual scene of pillage and destruction was going on. Much valuable private property was stolen or destroyed, and it was scarcely safe for the few inhabitants who remained to venture out of their houses.

At length, in April, the final overthrow of the Confederacy occurred, and the citizens of Charleston commenced by degrees to return, their hopes blasted and their fortunes gone, to their once beautiful home, now so sadly changed.

It is difficult to picture the condition of the city at this time. A considerable portion of it was in ruins, and every resource by which it might be built up again, and its trade and commerce revived, seemed hopelessly gone. We have had frequent occasion to allude to the great fire of 1861, but as yet have not mentioned any of the particulars of it. This fire, the most destructive Charleston has ever known, began in the large sash and blind factory of W. P. Russell & Co., near the foot of Hasel street, about half-past eight o'clock, on Wednesday night, December 11, 1861. The wind was blowing strongly from the north north-east, and the flames were quickly communicated to the adjoining buildings, and in a short time the fire had made such headway that all efforts to stay its progress were vain. In a broad line extending from the foot of Hasel street, on the Cooper River, to the end of Tradd street, on the Ashley, scarcely a building escaped. Among the public buildings destroyed were the Circular Church, the Institute Hall, St. Andrew's Hall, St. Finbar's Cathedral, and St. Peter's Church. The number of persons who sustained loss was near four hundred. The burnt district covered an area of five hundred and forty acres, and the loss of property variously estimated at from five to seven millions of dollars.

As may be supposed, nothing was ever attempted towards repairing the damage during the four years of war which followed, and the various fires which occurred during the shelling of the city, and at its evacuation, laid waste nearly as much more.

But this was by no means all the loss that the city had sustained; the entire banking capital was gone, the insurance companies were insolvent, and private capital, of course, in very nearly the same condition. The railroads which communicated with the city were all worn out, and in some cases destroyed, while the steamship lines had long been disused, and the few vessels which were owned in Charleston converted to other uses.

Under these circumstances, the task of re-opening the business of the city seemed absolutely hopeless, but the energy, courage, and endurance, which had characterized the people of Charleston through the dangers of the war, did not desert them in the greater trials of this time, and they boldly faced the difficulties before them; with what success, the present condition of the city shows.

The history of Charleston for the ten years which have passed since the war, is simply that of a people struggling against difficulties, and overcoming them one by one, until now we see a large part of the waste places built up, trade and commerce re-established, the old industries resumed, and even some new ones introduced, so that it is evident to the most superficial observer, that a very few more years are needed to restore the city to its former prosperity; and this opinion will be confirmed by an examination of the various branches of industry.

It is not within the scope of this sketch to enter into a statistical account of the business of the city, but the statements and figures which we give below can be relied on as being as nearly as possible accurate, and can be confirmed and amplified by reference to the reports of the various branches of trade. It must be remembered that the business year commences in Charleston on the first of September; the current year, therefore, is not included in our statements.

The banking capital of Charleston now amounts to $2,750,000.

The receipts of cotton at the port of Charleston from September 1, 1873, to August 31, 1874, were 438,718 bales.

The receipts of rice for the same time were 43,967 tierces. Of naval stores, about 225,683 barrels. Lumber is another important branch of trade at this port. The exports for the period above referred to were 19,568,091 feet.

There are five phosphate companies in active operation in Charleston; their works are located on the Cooper and Ashley rivers, within about five miles of the city. The manufacture of commercial fertilizers gives employment to upwards of $12,000,000 of capital. During the year 1864, 18,000 tons of crude phosphate were consumed by the Charleston companies, and the total exports and consumption reached the astonishing amount of 112,515 tons.

The cultivation of garden produce, in the neighborhood of Charleston, began in 1865 or 1866, when about 28,000 packages were shipped to the North. In 1871-72, the number of packages was 101,629, and in 1874, 149,757 packages were shipped from this port.

In addition to the business in the staple articles of Southern produce, Charleston has a larger jobbing trade in groceries, provisions, dry goods, medicines, and clothing, than is enjoyed by any other city in the South Atlantic States. The annual sales amount to $25,000,000, and experience has proved that the merchants of the interior of the State find it to their advantage to purchase their supplies in Charleston, rather than at the North.

Local manufactures have also progressed rapidly. The iron-works, five in number, give employment to upwards of three hundred hands, and more than a half million of capital. All of these establishments have founderies attached, in which the heaviest castings are made.

The South Carolina Railroad workshops have successfully attempted the manufacture of locomotive engines, which have proved quite equal to those made at the best Northern manufactories.

To Mr. John F. Taylor, the principal of the largest of these machine shops, belongs the honor of the invention of the hydraulic cotton press, which is acknowledged to be superior to any formerly in use, and has been adopted in several of the largest cities in the country.

There are seven cotton presses in Charleston, which prepare for shipment all of the cotton exported.

In addition to the manufactures above named, there are several sash and blind factories, which supply the city and the whole surrounding country, and a new branch of industry has been opened, in the establishment of a manufactory of ready-made houses, where all the parts of a house are made by machinery and fitted together; they are then taken apart and shipped to any part of the country, so arranged that the commonest carpenter can put them together and erect a neat dwelling.

Three lines of street railway traverse the city. The City Railway Company runs two, starting from the Battery, the lines run up Meeting street to Wentworth, where they divide, one going through Wentworth to Rutledge, and through Rutledge street and Rutledge Avenue to Sheppard street; the other, continuing up Meeting to Calhoun street, thence to King, through King to the same terminus. The Enterprise Railway has its lower terminus at the foot of East Bay, and follows that street to Calhoun, thence to Washington, and through Chapel, Elizabeth and John streets, to Meeting street, and is continued as far up as the entrance to Magnolia Cemetery, three miles from the Court House. This company proposes to establish a freight line from the farms on the neck, and the South Carolina and North-Eastern Railroad depots, to the several wharves along East Bay.

The facilities for transportation to and from Charleston are excellent. The South Carolina, North-Eastern, and Savannah and Charleston Railroads, connect with all points North and South, and when the Spartanburg and Asheville Railroad is completed, which promises to be in a short time, there will be full communication with the West and North-West, which cannot fail to add greatly to the commerce of the city.

The Steamship lines are admirably conducted and do a flourishing business; there are two lines to New York, and one each to Philadelphia, Baltimore, and Boston, besides the steamers which ply between Charleston and Georgetown, Beaufort, and other points along the coast of the State.

These are a few among the many advantages which Charleston enjoys as a commercial emporium. It remains for us now to notice some of the public buildings, whose erection marks a returning prosperity and some of the points of interest in and around the city.

The Academy of Music supplies the place of the old Charleston Theatre, on Meeting street, destroyed by the great fire. It is a very ornamental and admirably arranged little theatre, with a capacity for seating about twelve hundred persons; in proportion to the building, the stage is a very fine one, being forty feet deep, fifty-three feet wide, and fifty-one feet high. The building stands at the corner of King and Market streets, and has a front of sixty-feet, is two hundred and thirty-one feet deep, and seventy-five feet

Photo. by Barnard. *Eng. by Photo. Eng. Co., N. Y.*

ACADEMY OF MUSIC.

high. It was built for a mammoth dry goods store, the most extensive Charleston ever had, and its original cost was one hundred and sixty thousand dollars. In 1869, it was purchased by Mr. John Chadwick, a Northerner residing in Charleston, and the interior remodelled, making the theatre, two large halls, and a fine store on the first floor opening on King street.

The property has lately been purchased by Mr. John E. Owens, himself an actor, and there is every prospect that the theatre will always be occupied by a good company of actors.

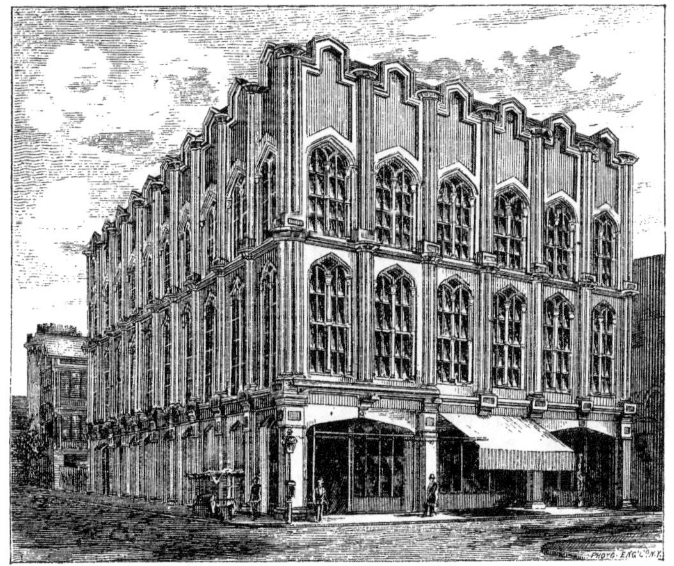

Photo. by Barnard. *Eng. by Photo. Eng. Co., N. Y.*

MASONIC TEMPLE.

The Masonic Temple, at the southeast corner of King and Wentworth streets, was erected by the Masonic fraternity for their meetings, and is arranged for the purpose. The first floor is occupied by three fine stores fronting on King street; in rear of these, on Wentworth street, is the main entrance to the second floor, which consists of a large hall, with one or two committee rooms; above this, on the third floor, are the smaller lodge rooms.

The United States Court House is situated on the west side of Meeting street, between Broad and Tradd, and is a very handsome three story building, recessed somewhat from the street, and having a neatly laid out garden in front. It was erected before the war by the Carolina Club, at that time one of the wealthiest in America, and was perfectly adapted for the comfort and entertainment of the members. After the war, the Club had lost all their funds, and the building was sold to the United States Government, and arranged for its present uses.

The new German Lutheran Church is situated on King street, opposite the Citadel. It is a very handsome building in the Gothic style, and speaks well for the enterprise and liberality of the German citizens.

Among the relics of early days in Carolina stands the Parish Church of St. Andrew's. This Parish was laid off in 1706, and a plain brick church built. In 1723 this was added to, making it in the form of a cross, forty feet long by fifty-two wide, with a handsome chancel twelve feet deep and twenty-four feet wide; it was neatly finished and had commodious pews. At the west end was a gallery, originally intended for those who had no pews, but afterwards appropriated to the colored people. At the east end was a large window, and another on each side of the communion table. This church was destroyed by fire, and rebuilt in 1764, and now remains one of the few which have escaped the vicissitudes of two revolutions.

Photo. by Barnard. *Eng. by Photo. Eng. Co., N. Y.*

NEW GERMAN CHURCH.

Before the war the Parish of St. Andrew's was quite prosperous, and there were many fine residences and rich farms in it; but it suffered severely, and the destruction of the bridge across the Ashley, by rendering communication with the city more difficult, has retarded its revival. The country, however, is beautiful, and well repays the trouble of a trip into it.

But by far the most interesting spot in the neighborhood of Charleston is the old Church of St. James'

Photo. by Barnard. *Eng. by Photo. Eng. Co., N. Y.*

OLD GOOSECREEK CHURCH.

Goosecreek, situated in the midst of a beautiful country, surrounded by many objects which excite the interest of the traveller, and connected by many associations with the history of the State in all its stages.

This has the advantage, too, of being easily accessible from the city. Taking the North-Eastern

Railroad, the excursionist is landed at Porcher's Station, fifteen miles from Charleston, on the grounds of the Otranto Club. This beautiful place, with its delightful residence, was once the property of the well known botanist, Dr. Garden, the correspondent of Linnæus, and after whom the great naturalist named our beautiful Gardenia.

A walk of about a mile takes us across Goose-creek bridge, along a winding road, to the church, a handsome rough cast brick building, a short distance from the creek. It has four arched windows and a door on each side, with a cherub in stucco, on each keystone; over the west door is a pelican feeding her young; at the east end is a large window, in front of which is the chancel, in which stand the altar, pulpit, and reading desk; over this window the Royal Arms of England still stand in high relief. The sides of the altar are ornamented with four Corinthian pilasters supporting a cornice, and between them are tables of the Decalogue, Apostles' Creed, and Lord's Prayer. The roof is supported by four Doric columns, and on the walls are several marble tablets, in memory of the early members of the congregation. Among them, one commemorates the virtues of the Hon. Ralph Izard, for many years one of the leading men of the State, and a gentleman of great ability and high culture.

A short distance from the church, on the other side of the main road, is a farm, known as "The Oaks," from the magnificent avenue of those trees by which it is approached. No one should leave the neighborhood without visiting this avenue. The trees are said to have been planted by one of the very earliest settlers, and are, consequently, near two hundred years old; they have attained great size, and for nearly a quarter of a mile form a continuous arch over the broad road; the dark foliage of the live oak, festooned with grey moss, renders the effect inexpressibly grand.

Charleston would be incomplete without her charming places of resort, Moultrieville, Mount Pleasant, and Summerville; the former occupies the historic ground of Sullivan's Island. The Island had become quite a fashionable resort before the war, and every summer presented a scene of much gayety. A fine hotel, the "Moultrie House," stood on the front beach, and was constantly filled with visitors; there were many fine residences, besides the large number of houses put up for temporary use, but the military operations demolished them, and at the end of the war there were not more than three houses standing on the whole Island. Since that time the growth has been astonishing; there are now four hundred houses on Moultrieville, a considerable portion of them handsome and substantial residences, completely finished in every respect, and it is estimated that not less than a half million of dollars has been spent in building.

In rear of Fort Moultrie, near the sally-port, a simple stone slab marks the grave of Oceola, the Seminole chief, whose sufferings while a prisoner there excited much sympathy. The killing of Gen.

Photo. by Barnard. *Eng. by Photo. Eng. Co., N. Y.*

OCEOLA'S GRAVE.

Thompson, the United States Indian agent, by him, brought about the second Seminole war, and in it he played a conspicuous part. For a long time he displayed great ability, as well as daring, in conducting the struggle against superior forces, but at length, on the 23d of October, 1837, while holding a conference under a flag of truce with Gen. Jesup, near St. Augustine, he was treacherously seized and sent to Fort Moultrie; there he was not treated with severity, and was, generally, permitted to walk about the Island, but he could not stand restraint, and literally

Photo. by Barnard. *Eng. by Photo. Eng. Co., N. Y.*

BIRD'S-EYE VIEW OF SULLIVAN'S ISLAND.

pined away, until death released him from his sufferings, on the 31st of January, 1838.

Each year more families are taking up their residence there for the summer, and thus finding an agreeable retreat from the city without the expense and trouble of going far away from home; and even from the interior of the State persons are coming to enjoy the salubrious climate and the many pleasures which the island affords.

The beach, nearly a hundred yards wide at low water, firm and shelving very gently, extends a distance of over three miles, and furnishes a delightful drive.

A splendid surf rolls in with the rising tide, and the tides and currents are so much to be depended on that Sullivan's Island is recognized as one of the safest, as well as one of the pleasantest places for sea-bathing along the entire Atlantic coast.

A street railway has lately been established, running from the Ferry wharf nearly to the end of the inhabited portion of the island; and this, with the improvements which have been made in the streets, has rendered travel very easy and pleasant.

The situation of the island, at the entrance of the harbor, is beautiful. One standing on the beach has to the east a view of the limitless extent of the ocean; before him lies Fort Sumter, and beyond it the shores of Morris' and James' Islands; while to the west stands the city, its fine buildings and graceful spires rising from the bay.

Sullivan's Island is endeared to every Charlestonian by his pride in the noble old fort which is so connected with the glory of the State in its two revolutions, and by the recollection of many happy days spent there; and to the stranger it is sure to be interesting, not only from its history, but also from the many pleasures which may be had in the way of fishing, surf-bathing, driving on the beach, etc.

Mount Pleasant, with its high bluff of yellow sand, and its background of dark foliage, forms a very pretty picture. This village was originally a summer resort for the planters of Christ Church Parish, but its healthy climate and pleasant situation soon induced a number of the business men of the city to adopt it as a retreat. Although not possessing the fine beach and surf of Sullivan's Island, it gets as much of the cool sea-breeze, and has the advantage of easy access to the surrounding country, affording pretty walks and drives, and during the winter season, a fine field for the sportsman.

The resources of this locality are as yet far from being developed. Already market gardening has become an important branch of industry in the neighborhood, the easy water communication with the city enabling the farmers to compete successfully with those on Charleston Neck, but the thing which will one day make Mount Pleasant a place of importance, is its peculiar fitness for the establishment of manufactories. Large cotton and other factories, which could not be conveniently located in the city itself, would here have ample room for the accommodation, in a healthy locality, of hundreds of operatives, and the perfectly easy access to the shipping of the port would render their being out of the city rather an advantage than otherwise. There can be little doubt that, as Charleston continues to grow, and the necessity of home manufacture becomes more evident, this plan, which has several times already been discussed, will be carried into execution.

Perhaps the most interesting spot at present in this little village is the soldiers' burying-ground. It contains about an acre of ground, in an elevated situation, and here lie buried not only the remains of Confederate and Federal soldiers, who died, or were killed, during the late war, but also those of several of the State troops, who died during the war of 1812. To the memory of these last a monument was erected many years ago, which still stands, and, though in a somewhat dilapidated condition, is the most conspicuous object in the burial ground. It is built of brick, and the upper part is a pyramid, which rests on a square foundation, on two of the sides of which marble slabs are let in, while the other two have been covered with white plaster, to resemble the marble. One of the slabs bears the following inscription: "On the 18th of June, 1812, the United States of America declared war against Great Britain. At the first sound of the trumpet the patriot soldiers who sleep beneath this monument flew to the standard of liberty. Here they fell beneath the scythe of death. The sympathies of the brave, the tear of the stranger, and the slow dirges of the camp, attended them to their tomb:

> "How sleep the brave who sink to rest,
> With all their country's wishes blest,
> The laurel leaf of shining green
> Will still around their tomb be seen."

The other side is inscribed to the memory of thirteen soldiers, of the third regiment of State troops.

Scattered around this monument, are the graves of some fifty or sixty Confederate soldiers.

Mount Pleasant and Sullivan's Island are easily reached by the boats of the Mount Pleasant and Sullivan's Island Ferry Company, which make frequent daily trips; this line is doing so well, that it is proposed soon to provide commodious and fast boats, such as are in use on the northern ferries.

Although spoken of as summer resorts, these two places are worth visiting at any time. The woods around Mount Pleasant are always beautiful, and in the spring are a mass of jessamines, whose fragrance fill the air.

The island is to a great extent deserted in the winter, but the sea breeze is always mild, and on a clear, cold day, nothing is more exhilarating than a brisk walk on the beach.

Contrasted with these two seaside resorts, is Summerville, about twenty-two miles from Charleston, on the line of the South Carolina Railroad, and in the midst of the pine woods. It is situated on a ridge which extends across from the Cooper to the Ashley River, and which is remarkable for its healthfulness. The climate is very agreeable; in winter being out of the influence of the east winds, which frequently prevail on the coast, the temperature is mild and equable, and in summer, though the days are warm, a delicious coolness pervades the atmosphere at night which ensures refreshing sleep. From these causes it is particularly beneficial to invalids, or persons convalescing from illness. The village has been settled a very long time, but, like most places of the kind, has grown slowly. It has now, however, reached quite a respectable size. The houses are built far apart, so that each one is perfectly private, and like a country residence.

The many advantages which Summerville possesses are being rapidly realized, and each year the popula tion is increasing. There are several excellent boarding houses, which are generally full. Churches of all the religious denominations, good schools and a well supplied market furnish all the requisites for comfortable and pleasant living, and many families, induced by these advantages, and by the cheapness of house rents, are taking up their residence there. As the South Carolina Railroad runs special trains for the accommodation of the residents, it is perfectly convenient for business men, who find it a great relief, after the fatigues of a day in the city, to retreat to the quiet of Summerville.

The country around abounds with game, and the Summerville men have always been renowned as hunters. Although situated, as we have said, in a pine-barren, there are many pretty walks and drives about the village, and on the banks of the Ashley, about four miles off, some spots of great beauty. The most interesting of these is Newington, once an elegant country seat, now a picturesque ruin. Approaching from Summerville by a rather uninteresting pineland road, the scene suddenly changes, and we find ourselves in the midst of a dense growth of live oaks, magnolias, and other trees, denoting the neighborhood of the river; passing through a belt of these we come upon an open space, in which stand the walls of the once splendid mansion, almost hidden by a dense growth of vines and creeping plants.

Besides Newington, there are in this neighborhood the remnants of several other seats, which were occupied by wealthy men in the days when this part of the country was more resorted to than it is at present. The question is frequently asked by strangers, how it is that these places, which were evidently at one time noble residences, are now entirely deserted. There are two causes. In the first place, it is rather a remarkable fact, that the climate of the country seems to have changed, and places which were once quite healthy, are now altogether the reverse. It was formerly a common thing for persons to go to the plantations along the Cooper, Ashley, and Santee Rivers, to spend the summer. Fifty years ago Newington, for instance, would have been regarded as an agreeable summer retreat; now any person who should venture to spend a night there during the summer months, would be almost sure of an attack of chills and fever.

But, besides that, this part of the country is no longer profitable for cultivation. Sea Island cotton and rice belong to the sea-board, and upland cotton is more profitably cultivated in the interior of the State. There is no doubt that in time the facilities which this part of the State enjoys for stock-raising, small farming, and other branches of agricultural industry, will be appreciated and developed, but in the mean time it remains comparatively uninhabited.

With these three delightful resorts, Charleston enjoys advantages possessed by few cities in this country; the citizens can at a small expense, and without the necessity of giving up business or breaking up the family circle, obtain relaxation from the confinement of the city, or a healthy retreat in seasons of sickness; and when a freer communication is established with the mountain regions of South and North Carolina, an opportunity will be afforded to those who desire more completely to change scene and climate, to do so easily and comfortably, and without going much beyond the boundaries of their own State.

As the advantages become more appreciated, they add largely to the material prosperity of the city. Money made here is kept in circulation in and around the city instead of being spent in distant places. Charleston mechanics build the houses, which are in demand, the supplies are all obtained from the city, and a large number of persons are given employment in various capacities.

The facilities which Charleston enjoys for communication with the outer world are too great to permit her people to become provincial or narrow-minded, and their growing ability to live within themselves, and on their own resources, cannot be too highly valued.

Magnolia Cemetery is one of the features of the city which cannot fail to be interesting to the stranger as well as to the resident of the city, to whom it is endeared by many touching associations.

It is situated just beyond the limits of the city, three miles from the Court House. Since the completion of the Enterprise Railway, as far as the entrance to the avenue leading to the cemetery, it is very easy of access. We enter first Bethany Cemetery. This is the burial ground of the German population, as any one will at once perceive by the inscriptions on the tombstones, which are all in the German language. The solemn and touching words, "Her ruhet in Gott," greet the eye at every step, impressing the imagination with religious awe, and forming, as it were, an ever present consecration of the hallowed spot. This cemetery is beautifully kept and its white gravelled walks shining amid the green shrubbery and the blooming flowers, and under the aged oaks, illustrate well how nature is improved by art.

Leaving this cemetery we come to the main entrance to Magnolia, through a massive gate, with a porter's lodge just within. A large bell is suspended from a scaffolding near by, which is solemnly tolled on the approach of a funeral procession.

Standing in the gateway, you can, about a hundred yards distant on your left, across the still waters of the serpentine, see the small Gothic Chapel of the Cemetery, where the burial service is sometimes read. Passing in, and keeping on the right, you soon see an array of a score or more of white wooden head-boards, that look like ghostly sentinels at the gates of death. These mark the resting place of the Federal soldiers who have died in Charleston. Just beyond these is the Confederate burying ground. Side by side and rank on rank, as when they charged the bristling breastworks of the enemy, now lie these patriot soldiers of a vanquished country, in sweet oblivion of the stupendous ruin that has crushed the land of their nativity and love. Of that crowd of hillocks, there are some that have no mark to tell who lies beneath. Their occupants belong to the vast throng of the unknown dead—unknown, yet unforgotten, living ever in the hearts of the people whom they died to defend. Orators have pronounced their eulogy, flowers have decked their graves, and the incense of their praise has gone up to heaven on the music of the voices of the people, but it remains for the historian's pen to embalm their memory in the language of truthful commendation, and for posterity to accord that meed of lasting fame which valor and endurance, when prompted by noted motives, and exercised in a holy cause, must ever win. A granite pedestal, intended to bear an appropriate monument, marks the centre of the ground.

Passing from the Confederate burying ground, we enter the Catholic cemetery. This is truly a city of the dead. A broad, white street runs through the middle from east to west, in the central and highest point of which is erected a huge black wooden cross. On each side the lots are laid out in various forms—square, circular, semi-circular, oval, etc. Most of the lots are nicely kept, and the well-trimmed cedars and shrubbery, and the numerous roses and other flowers, make them look like little gardens.

The sign of the cross consecrates every grave, wooden crosses being erected where there is no other head board, and marble crosses carved on all the upright monuments, while a representation of a cross is engraved on the horizontal slabs.

At the eastern end of this cemetery you catch through the openings of the shrubbery that border the marsh, occasional glimpses of the river; but by passing a break in the hedge that here divides the Roman Catholic from the Protestant portion of the grounds, and walking a few steps to what is, we believe, the south-eastern point of Magnolia, just below the lot of the Kerrison family, you can, on a bright day, obtain a most magnificent view of the city and harbor. The city spires of St. Michael's, St. Philip's, Grace Church, the Citadel Square Baptist Church, the new German Church, and even the low steeple of Flinn's Church, and the cupola of the Orphan House, are clearly defined against the sky; the dim smoke curls up from the chimneys of the founderies and steam mills, and trails far behind the flying locomotives. The residences in the north-eastern part of the city can be recognized, and beyond them can be seen the clustering masts of the vessels at the wharves. The sun glances on the blue ripples of the waters of the bay, while Sumter looms up in the distance, a stern memento of the past. Vessels, with white sails, pass to and fro, and the row-boats, with their singing oarsmen, while the blue pines, glittering sands, white houses, and low forts of James' Island, Morris Island, Sullivan's Island, and Christ Church, form a charming back ground or border, and Castle Pinckney occupies a prominent place in the foreground.

Turning back from this view to the cemetery, we come upon many elegant monuments, now marking the resting place of distinguished citizens, but space only permits the mention of one or two; and first we have the

WILLIAM WASHINGTON MONUMENT.

One of the attractions of these beautiful grounds is this elegant testimonial to one of the foremost men of the Revolutionary army. Col. Washington came to South Carolina, under assignment, as commander of cavalry, and made a great name as an active and brave partisan leader. During the war he met Miss Jane Elliott, of Charleston, who improvised for his cavalry regiment a flag, by cutting out from a rich drawing-room chair the crimson brocade adorning the back of it, which had the merit of being very distinct in color and handy in size. She became Mrs. Washington, and, in 1827, presented her husband's battle flag to the Washington Light Infantry of Charleston, at the solicitation of Col. George Warren Cross, Capts. R. B. Gilchrist and Henry Ravenel, all members of the corps. The ceremony took place at the Battery residence, corner of Church street, and Sergt. Henry S. Tew was the first color-bearer, and the scene is still remembered by several surviving members of that parade. This venerated relic is the only one which can be traced directly to the battle-fields of the American Revolution, in the custody of a military corps, and wherever borne evokes the

Photo. by Barnard. *Eng. by Photo. Eng. Co., N. Y.*

THE WM. WASHINGTON MONUMENT.

wildest enthusiasm, the latest instance being on the occasion of the visit of the Washington Light Infantry to the Bunker Hill Centennial, in Boston, June, 1875. Strange, how a very trifling incident produces, after many years, a marked result. That flag presentation of 19th April, 1827, brought a response thirty years afterwards. In the midst of the memorable festivities of the semi-centennial celebration of the corps, 22d February, 1857, ex-Commander Ravenel proposed that, in honor of Colonel and Mrs. Washington, the Company erect a suitable monument to both, which was voted *unanimously.* Col. E. B. White asked the privilege of being allowed to furnish the design, which was contracted for, and carved in Charleston, by Mr. W. T. White. It is of Italian marble, and executed with great taste and skill. The State Society of the Cincinnati, through a committee, consisting of James Simons, D. H. Hamilton, Wm. H. Peronneau, Evan Edwards, and David Ramsay, asked that the society be allowed to furnish an iron fence for the enclosing of the lot, which was acceded to by the company. The doorposts are brass cannon, presented by Gov. Alston, of South Carolina, from the State Arsenal, both of revolutionary date, as are also the sabres crossed over the doorway. The fence is of wrought iron, made in this city, by Mr. Merker, and the whole affair is well calculated to do honor to the prominent corps to whom it belongs; while no American can see it without a feeling of pride and satisfaction.

Near the Washington Monument, stands another costly shaft, erected by the Washington Light Infantry to the one hundred and thirteen dead companions of their three companies, serving in the war between the States from Charleston; of which about forty per cent. "perished in battle, in hospital, or on

the weary wayside—officers and men, they were of the very flower of this ancient city, her young hope and fair renown."

The Eutaw Flag, as it is familiarly called, is of heavy crimson brocade silk, and having been in existence nearly a century, showed so many signs of wear, that, in 1874, it was quilted on to a similar piece of crimson silk, and the work is so beautifully done by a lady—W. L. I.—as to preserve it, for another century, in active use. It is mounted in the Roman style. Surmounting the staff is the eagle, with wings ready for his flight; and below, the classic initials S. P. Q. R.; cord and tassels of gold bullion. It is displayed on parades of 22d February and 28th June every year, and not otherwise, except by special orders for some unusual occasion.

The company has a large pension list, and distributes about a thousand dollars a year to the widows and children of their dead comrades. The pension certificates are enclosed, on the first of January, to the pensioners, who have only to endorse the quarterly coupons attached, at the date of maturity, and send it to the bank to be cashed—a delicate way

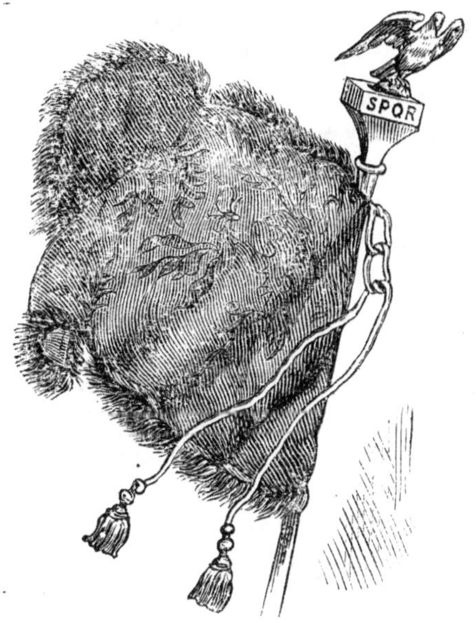

EUTAW FLAG.

of avoiding calls on the treasurer, which would be inconvenient to ladies—while the amount to be received during the year is at the same time communicated.

The corps has thus honored the memory of their dead and has been ever mindful of their responsibility to the widow and the fatherless. This is the secret of their widespread popularity, and explains the generous responses elicited at the late grand Easter fair.

The next monument that we will notice, is that of Hugh S. Legare, one of the handsomest in the Cemetery. It is a beautiful column of white marble, upon a pedestal of the same, tastefully ornamented with the sculptured coats of arms of the United States and South Carolina. No pen sketch can give an accurate idea of its graceful beauty. It is inscribed "Hugh S. Legare, Attorney General and Acting Secretary of State of the United States, born January 2, 1797, died in Boston, June 20, 1843, aged 46 years." His remains were moved to this city and the monument was erected in 1857. In another place is inscribed, "South Carolina claims the remains of her gifted and cherished son." "This monument is erected to his memory by his sister, admirers and friends." South Carolina has produced few more able or more distinguished men than Hugh S. Legare, and it is extremely gratifying that so handsome a monument marks his tomb.

But it would be impossible to attempt to describe the many interesting and beautiful objects on these grounds. One must stroll through the smooth and shady walks and note them for himself.

Among our illustrations of the city churches we have had the French Protestant or Huguenot; there is so much of interest connected with this church, and with that part of the community by whom it was founded, and is still maintained, that we insert a more extended notice, feeling sure that it will be appreciated by the citizens of Charleston, as well as strangers, who come to visit the city and learn something of its history.

"The French Protestant Church of Charleston is one of four churches founded by the French Protestants who, on the Revocation of the Edict of Nantz, sought civil and religious liberty in that part of the Province of Carolina since known as South Carolina."* Originally it was styled "*L'Eglise Reformee Francaise de Charlestown*," and is now generally known as the Huguenot Church.

This church is nearly coeval with Charleston, and is one of the two oldest in it. Charleston was established at Oyster Point, the site on which it now is, in 1680, and in 1686 there was a French Protestant congregation in the town. In 1686—some months after the Revocation of the Edict of Nantz—the refugees from France began to arrive; and there was among the papers of the church, before the late war, a warrant for laying out certain lots in the town, and the certificate of admeasurement of the Surveyor-General, dated as early as the 9th December of that year, for a grant, "in order to the building of a church in behalf of the French Protestants of this Province." The will of Cæsar Moze, dated the 20th June, 1687, on record in the Secretary of State's office, confirms this statement of the early organization of this church. By it, he bequeathed to the church of the "Protestant French Refugees, in Charlestown," thirty-seven pounds, to assist in building a house of worship in the neighborhood of his plantation, on the eastern branch of Cooper River. Thus, it is certain that there was a French Protestant church in Charlestown about six years after the town was established here—and it was this church.

---

*Unpublished manuscript of the late Mr. Daniel Ravenel.

And, further, as to its antiquity, Chalmers enumerates certain laws enacted at a Parliament* held by Governor West, in 1682, one being "to promote the morality of a people who did not enjoy the instruction of a public ministry."† In December, 1686, a warrant had issued for laying out lots for a church for the French Protestants, and in June, 1687, the church of the "Protestant French Refugees in Charlestown" was the trustee of Cæsar Moze, for a certain pious purpose. It would appear from this measure that there was no organized public worship in the Province in 1682. This church was, therefore, among the first, if not the first, established in Charlestown. Within four or five years after the Provincial Parliament legislated to promote the morals of the people, being without a public ministry, this church was founded. Whether any other church was organized with a public ministry or worship in the interval between 1682 and 1687 history does not inform us.

They who are familiar with the religious character and habits of the Huguenots, will not be surprised by the promptness with which they organized and estab-

---

* Political Annals, Carroll's Collections, second volume, page 316.

† On the 26th May, 1682, an Act "for the observation of the Lord's day," and another "for the suppression of idle, drunken, and swearing persons inhabiting within this province," was adopted by the Parliament. These Acts have been lost; the titles alone remain on the statute book. Whether Chalmers refers here to one or both, cannot now be known. But Carroll tells us that he was, for several years, secretary to the Proprietors, and it is to be supposed that he was familiar with the statements and provisions of these laws.

lished their church in Charlestown.* They were unlike other immigrants to the Province. Fugitives from religious persecution, "they brought with them their holy men."† The invisible spiritual church was with them in their flight when they landed, wherever they made their home, whether in the town or in the wilderness, and when their journeyings were ended, they gave to it a visible habitation.

The early records of the church were lost in the fire which destroyed a large portion of Charleston, in 1740, and it is not known when the French Protestants built their first church, or where it was located. Tradition, however, has always associated it with the spot on which their descendants are worshipping to-day, and there is reason to believe that it was located here, not later than 1692, and probably two or three years earlier.

The site of the church, at the south-east corner of Church and Queen streets, was not the endowment of the Lords Proprietors, as is generally supposed. They endowed the church with the lots described in the warrant and certificate of admeasurement, already mentioned, lying in King street, between Broad and Tradd streets. This property was held as a glebe until 1871, when excessive taxation compelled the church to sell it. It was sold, except one house, for

* The Churches at their settlements on the Santee River, at Orange Quarter, and on St. John's Berkley, were organized with the same promptness.

† Simms.

which there was no purchaser, at an adequate price. Apart from the sacrifices of this enforced sale, the alienation of this benefaction and ancient glebe was a painful necessity in the history of the church. The parsonage in Church street, adjoining the church, was also sold.

The three other churches founded by the Refugees to the Province of Carolina, were located at their settlements in the country, and have long since been extinct. This church alone remains and maintains its distinctive character and worship. Indeed it is believed that this is the only church founded in the United States by the French Refugees which exists, to bear witness to their piety, constancy, and courage, to their religious heroism.

This church has been preserved despite its isolation, and notwithstanding the calamities it has suffered during one century and three-fourths of another. The generations which have come successively into life, in the course of these long years, have watched over it with filial love and veneration, and it has been their desire to maintain it as it was established, in the faith of their forefathers, with their form of worship and in their tongue. The effort to execute these purposes had been persistent, but unsuccessful, and some fifty years ago it was thought expedient to relax it so far as related to the language in which the services were conducted; and the liturgy was translated into English.

There is a tradition that the church erected by the refugees was burnt in the fire of 1740, when the records were lost. The account of this fire in the *South Carolina Gazette*, two days after it occurred, makes no mention of this, and there is, probably, no foundation for it. But the church which was standing in 1796 was destroyed in the disastrous fire of the 13th of June of that year. It was rebuilt. Unhappily the death of the pastor, the Rev. Mr. Bouedillion, followed quickly on this misfortune, and the congregation became scattered.

After several ineffectual efforts to revive the church, it was reopened in June, 1843, for the summer, under the ministry of the Reverend and Venerable Daniel DuPre; the English translation of the Liturgy being used; and, in the autumn, in accordance with a purpose always entertained, it was resolved to continue the services regularly and permanently. But the church was small and inconveniently arranged, and it was necessary to rebuild it. This was done, and the Rev. Charles Wallace Howard was called to the pastorate. On the 11th May, 1845, the new edifice was dedicated. And here have worshipped, since that time, many descendants of the Huguenot fathers. The Rev. Charles S. Vedder is now the pastor.

The tenets of the Church are set forth in the Articles entitled "Confession of Faith made by common consent of the Reformed Churches of the Kingdom of France," in 1539. Its worship is Liturgical. The Liturgy is described, on its title page, as "Translated from the Liturgy of the Churches of Neufchatel and Vallangin; Editions of 1737 and 1772; with some occasional prayers, carefully selected."

The present church was designed and its erection superintended by Edward B. White, Esq. The architecture is Gothic, simple and chaste in character. The position of the organ in a gallery at the east end, and the arrangement of the church, below and to the front of it, with the Decalogue, the Lord's Prayer and the Creed on tablets against the wall on either side, is peculiarly tasteful and happy, and will arrest the attention of the stranger as he enters. The gallery at the west end has always been appropriated to the use of colored worshippers. The walls are embellished with monuments, of considerable elegance, to the memory of the founders of some of the Huguenot families of South Carolina. That dedicated to the Rev. Elias Prioleau, is peculiarly interesting and deserves notice. He was minister of the Church at Pons, in France, until it was demolished in April, 1686, when he came to Carolina. It is believed that Mr. Prioleau, and the Rev. Florent Philipe Truillard, were associated in the ministry of this church, and were its first Pastors. The walls of the church were greatly damaged in the bombardment of the city in the late war, but fortunately (miraculously) neither the monuments nor the organ were injured. The chandeliers were taken from the church, after the evacuation of the city, by persons unknown.

The communion plate and many valuable records of the church were sent to Cheraw for safety, and were lost when Sherman's army passed through that place.

The cemetery around the church is not extensive,

and the tombs and grave stones are few, when its antiquity is considered. Many, probably, were destroyed when the church was burnt; others were mutilated by shells in the late war. Many of those that remain bear upon them names of families familiar in the history and in the social life of this State. Perhaps, very probably, Judith Manigault rests from her sorrows and troubles here. She who, after sufferings and privations unparalleled, in her flight from France and in her new home, recorded thus her pious submission to the Divine will. "God accomplished great things in our favor by giving us the strength necessary to support these trials."

Among the most important charitable institutions of Charleston is

THE CONFEDERATE HOME.

This noble charity, justly the pride of the city and State, gives shelter to the mothers, widows, daughters, and other female relatives and dependents of Confederate soldiers, who had been left homeless by the death or ruin of those who fought for the "lost cause."

Soon after the close of the war, a lady of this city was impressed with the importance of establishing such an institution. While ruminating the importance of the subject, she chanced to be in Baltimore, and visited the Home there. In conversation with a widowed inmate, she mentioned her desire for such a Home in Charleston; the poor widow immediately

Photo. by Barnard. *Eng. by Photo. Eng. Co., N. Y.*

ORPHAN HOUSE. [See page 43.]

handed one dollar to the visitor, who declined the gift. "What," said the widow, "do you reject my gift because it is so small?" "Oh, no," was the reply, and this one dollar given by a pensioner on public charity, was the beginning of the Charleston Home. The lady returned to Charleston, and after a conference with friends, determined to make a beginning. It was decided to take a house, the rent of which was one thousand eight hundred dollars. The proprietor reasonably demanded security for the rent; the lady in question immediately mortgaged her house and lot as security; noble gentlemen stepped forward and paid the rent as it fell due. Such was the beginning of the Charleston Home. Now it sustains forty widowed inmates and sixty pupils. It is not a charity, but the fulfilment of an obligation. The names of some of the most distinguished families of South Carolina are found among the inmates of this noble institution—inmates from all sections of the State.

The Home has been bought, but not paid for in full; the last instalment falls due in April, 1876, and it is hoped that the friends of the Home will aid in securing the requisite amount. An association of ladies carry on the Home, and the management of the institution is in the hands of thirteen ladies, elected from this Ladies' Association annually, and known as the "Board of Control." The Board, from its own number, elects a president, vice-president, corresponding and recording secretaries, and a treasurer The more material, or monetary, aid comes from the "Gen-

Photo. by Barnard. *Eng. by Photo. Eng. Co., N. Y.*
ST. ANDREW'S CHURCH. [See page 104.]

tlemen's Auxiliary Association." This body, consisting of gentlemen residing in all parts of the State, and some few outside of its limits, contribute the entire amount of its income, ten dollars from each member, to the support of the Home; and, through the medium of its executive committee, extend aid and counsel in matters of management and advice, when called upon by the Board of Control.

The inmates of the Home, other than those in the "school department," have comfortable rooms furnished them rent free, or at nominal prices, and are never allowed to suffer for the necessaries of life. It is to the "school department," however, that we must look for the most enduring and substantial benefits of this noble offering to the loved memories of those who wore the "grey." Sixty girls being educated,

Photo. by Barnard. *Eng. by Photo. Eng. Co., N. Y.*

ZION CHURCH.

either as beneficiaries, or for very small annual payments, not only to be well educated and refined women, but, if necessary, to support themselves and those dependent upon them. The Home is complete from kitchen to sleeping apartments, and only the actual drudgery is performed by the servants, three in

Photo. by Barnard. *Eng. by Photo. Eng. Co., N. Y.*

HALF MOON BATTERY.

number. The house is large and commodious, well ventilated, and supplied with water and bath rooms on each floor, more economically conducted than, perhaps, any other institution in the South ; the girls are taught habits of punctuality, economy, and neatness; they learn the routine of house-keeping, and acquire the ease and graceful deportment of refined women. The touching story of the origin of this Home found its way into the newspapers. The eye of a wealthy American gentleman, Mr. Corcoran, of Washington, then in France, fell upon the statement, and his check for one thousand dollars, was immediately forwarded as a contribution to its support.

This noble Christian gentleman recently visited the Home, and was so much pleased after his inspection of its workings and management, that he contributed the handsome sum of five thousand dollars to its permanent fund. Those wishing to aid the Confederate Home, "can do so by contributions, small or large; by joining the Gentlemen's Auxiliary Association," and paying ten dollars annually, or two hundred dollars to become life members; or they may purchase scholarships for five hundred dollars, and nominate beneficiaries, subject to the approval of the Board of Control.

Mrs. M. A. Snowden, President Board of Control, or Mr. Henry A. Gourdin, "Gentlemen's Auxiliary Association, will be glad to give any information not contained in the above sketch, and will gratefully receive all contributions or subscriptions.

We have endeavored to point out the prominent

Photo. by Barnard. *Eng. by Photo. Eng. Co., N. Y.*

RESIDENCE OF F. J. PELZER, ESQ.

features of interest in and around Charleston, not only for the benefit of strangers, but also for the citizens themselves, a large number of whom are quite unaware of the resources of their own home. Since the war especially, when the struggle for existence has been all engrossing, many valuable public institutions have been neglected, not intentionally, but because they have been overlooked; and many sources of amusement and interest lost sight of, which would help our people to bear their labors more cheerfully, to entertain their friends from abroad more easily and pleasantly, and to avoid the necessity, when a little relaxation from business cares is needed, of taking an expensive and troublesome journey to obtain it.

Necessarily, in such a brief sketch, much has been omitted, both in the history and the description of Charleston, which would be interesting and instructive; but our chief object will have been accomplished, if we shall have succeeded in merely indicating the sources from which information and amusement may be obtained.

Photo. by Barnard. *Eng. by Photo. Eng. Co., N. Y.*

CAROLINA SAVINGS BANK.

OUR BUSINESS HOUSES.

Charleston has many business houses in various lines of trade, and we have selected a few of the principal ones for special notice. Commencing at the Post Office from which radiate East Bay and Broad streets, including between them the business section of the city, the first we notice in position, as well as in importance and amount of capital, is the banking house of

GEO. W. WILLIAMS & CO.

The house of Geo. W. Williams & Co. was established in Augusta, Ga., May 1st, 1842, under the firm name of Hand & Williams. The business, although small at the beginning, was by energy, push, and tact, made the largest in the South.

The firm confined itself steadily to a wholesale grocery business. The capital had increased to such an extent in ten years, the firm found it expedient to enlarge their field of operations. Mr. Williams being favorably impressed with Charleston, he visited that city for the purpose of establishing a wholesale grocery business, upon strictly temperance principles; this he did in 1852. The sales at Augusta and in Charleston rose from one hundred thousand dollars,

Photo. by Barnard. *Eng. by Photo. Eng. Co., N. Y.*

GROCERY HOUSE OF GEORGE W. WILLIAMS & CO.

to one million five hundred thousand dollars per annum, and the profits from ten thousand per annum, to more than one hundred thousand. The war put a stop to all trade, and the business was discontinued in 1862, but so judiciously was the capital invested, as to leave more than a million of dollars with which to begin business at the termination of the war.

Mr. Williams proceeded to Washington City, in the summer of 1865, via Hilton Head, for the purpose of procuring a charter for a National Bank. In the mean time he resumed his mercantile operations, bringing into his firm the following copartners: Geo. W. Williams, Edward C. Williams, James H. Taylor, William Birnie, Edwin Platt. Thus organized, the grocery business was re-established; and, in addition, a cotton factorage house in Charleston and one in New York. The firm commenced at once the erection of large brick warehouses in the "burnt district," for the storage of cotton and fertilizers.

The senior's mercantile duties were such as to prevent his taking charge of a bank, but he united with A. Simonds, E. W. Marshall, W. L. Trenholm and others, in establishing the "First National Bank, of Charleston," an institution which has paid to its stockholders more than twelve per cent. per annum since its organization.

In May, 1874, the firm celebrated its 32d anniversary. We extract from the Charleston *News and Courier* an interesting account of that celebration:

"Seldom has Charleston known a more pleasant and interesting gathering around the festive board than

Photo. by Barnard. *Eng. by Photo. Eng. Co., N. Y.*

CHARLESTON CROCKERY IMPORTING COMPANY.

that which met on Saturday afternoon, to celebrate at once the 32d anniversary of the great mercantile and banking house of George W. Williams & Co., and the inauguration of 'The Carolina Savings' Bank,' an addition to our banking facilities, which is the offspring of the energy of the distinguished head of the firm, and for which it is safe to predict a career as wonderfully prosperous as that of every other business enterprise launched under his auspices.

"The name of Geo. W. Williams & Co., long before the war, had become as familiar as household words to the commercial community of Charleston. The history of the house is a record of spotless probity, indomitable energy, remarkable tact and success, that has been as unvarying as it has been brilliant. Even more remarkable has been the individual career of Mr. Williams. He is emphatically a self-made man. During the third of a century that he has guided the fortunes of the firm, he has had no less than twenty-five partners, many of whom have retired with fortunes, while all have acquired a competency. The house, to-day, occupies a proud position among the great business firms of South Carolina.

"It is composed of six copartners, George W. Williams, William Birnie, J. R. Robertson, James Bridge, Jr., Frank E. Taylor, and R. S. Cathcart. It is worthy of note, that all of Mr. Williams' partners began as clerks in his house. The main establishment is on Hayne street, but the immense business of the firm requires the use of over a dozen large warehouses, many of which have been built since the war in dif ferent sections of the city. Such a business, of course, gives employment to a large clerical force, besides twenty drays, and about one hundred colored laborers.

"The Carolina Savings Bank, the inauguration of which was celebrated May 2, was chartered at the last session of the General Assembly, and begins business, with the following officers: Geo. W. Williams, President; Joseph R. Robertson, Vice-President; William E. Breese, Cashier. Directors: Geo. W. Williams, Joseph R. Robertson, Edward C. Williams, James Bridge, Jr., Frank E. Taylor, Robert S. Cathcart, Edward J. Gage."

On the first of May last, the Carolina Savings Bank was removed to the fine banking building of Geo. W. Williams & Co., located at No. 1 Broad street, opposite the old Post Office.

The stock of the Carolina Savings Bank is all owned by Geo. W. Williams & Co., and they guarantee all deposits made in the Bank.

The Charleston Crockery Importing Company, established and owned by Messrs. Geo. W. Williams & Co., and managed by W. G. Whilden, Esq., has been very successful.

Another important establishment is that of Messrs.

WALKER, EVANS & COGSWELL,

situated at 3 Broad street, and 109 East Bay. The building now occupied for the business was originally two stores, one on Broad street and one on East Bay, but a short time before the war the two were extended so as to form one large building, now fronting on Broad street, and running through, in an L shape, to East Bay. Entering on the Broad street front, we see immediately before us the sales room for Stationery and Blank Books. Here is a complete stock of everything needed in this line, of the choicest and most useful kinds. The blank books are all made in the establishment, and in this the firm are entirely independent of the North. This is the only concern in the South which, as far as we know, manufacture all the blank books which are sold upon their shelves. Turning down the East Bay arm of the store we see first the Folded Paper Department with its shelves well filled with the famous brands, R. E. Lee, Live Oak, Magnolia, Laurel; these are the trade names of the papers which are put up by this house:

We also see a goodly array of Herrings Fire Proof Safes, Walker, Evans & Cogswell being the agents for this manufacture.

Further down, we see thousands of shipping tags, which suggest the source from which come the numbers which meet our eyes at every railroad depot in the South, attached to the bags of Charleston fertilizers.

On the north side of this store is kept the reserve stock of blank books, which cannot find place on the west side of the Broad street front.

And here we see a capacious law blank case being put into position. On inquiry, we find that it is to hold the law blanks for Alabama, the trade in which

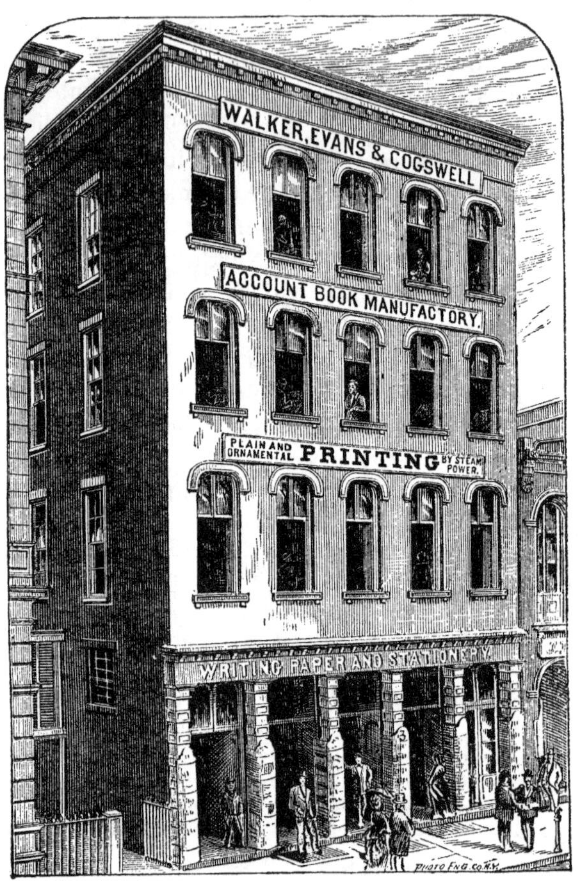

Photo. by Barnard. *Eng. by Photo. Eng. Co., N. Y.*

WALKER, EVANS & COGSWELL, 3 BROAD STREET.

the firm is largely engaged. They propose to keep a full stock of law forms for this State, in addition to their stock of South Carolina blanks. We know of none who are better able to do this business promptly, cheaply, and well. Their large resources give them a great advantage over all their competitors.

On the East Bay store, in the second story, is the stock room for the stock used in the various processes of printing and binding, piles of paper reaching to the ceiling meet our eyes all around, and it looks as if they had stock enough, and in great enough variety, to fill the largest orders, or please the most fastidious taste. In the extension of the building to the south, is located the steam engine which drives the machinery. It is a beautiful piece of mechanism, and as it turns upon its noiseless and unceasing labor, it seems indeed a thing of life. It was built by Messrs. James M. Eason & Brother, and reflects credit upon them. Near by is one of Sheridan's Power Paper Cutters. All jobs which require cutting before being passed to the workshops are here manipulated, and here also the finishing cuts are given.

In the second story, on Broad street front, is the ruling room—plenty of the best machinery and highly skilled labor, enables the ruling to be done with great promptness and care.

Back of the ruling room are the paging machines and monogram press, worked by girls—huge blank books were being paged, in which to keep the records of the merchant's earnings, some of which were to be

Photo. by Barnard. *Eng. by Photo. Eng. Co., N. Y.*

WALKER, EVANS & COGSWELL, 109 EAST BAY.

spent on monograming the fine papers for his wife and daughters.

Passing to the third story, we are in the printing office on the Broad street front, the large job composing room, alive with typos, whose quick hands are gathering the mechanical elements of learning, type, and putting them in intelligible shape. To the rear of this room is the book composing room, where the quiet is only broken by the click of the type as it drops into the composing stick.

The entire East Bay store, on this floor, is the press room. Driven by a long line of shafting, we see the most improved printing machinery of the age. Presses in every variety, and all of the most improved patterns, are used. We see in the various states of perfection all kinds of jobs, in black ink and in colored inks; law blanks, letter heads, bill heads, cards, almanacs, and fine books. We also are attracted by the novel sight of girls feeding the presses. They are all neat, active, and efficient, and we only regret that other firms have not followed the example of this, and opened for women employment other than the needle.

On the fourth story on the Broad street front and running back to the extreme South extension of the building, is the girl's room. Sewing books, stitching pamphlets, sewing huge bank books, and books for the store, were the fair daughters of Eve, neat, happy, and glad to work.

In the fifth story is another room for keeping the leathers, twines, and other book-binder's stock.

Stepping out to the fourth floor, we are again among the sterner sex, and in the bindery, which occupies the East Bay end of the building; men and boys all hard at work on tall piles of blank books of every description; one on a bank book for Charleston, another on a county book for Lee County, Ala. We see cutting machines, presses, and tools of the most approved make for doing the best work in the world.

And all this has been built up in the past few years. Sherman destroyed every vestige of the *ante bellum* machinery, and all is new.

ROBSON'S RANGE.

This engraving represents the commodious stores of J. N. Robson, Commission Merchant, No. 68 East Bay street, erected by him soon after the fire of 1870. This finely finished building forms a part of the old range in which he began business in 1839. These compact stores open on three streets, and afford one of the safest and most commodious warehouses in the city. The proprietor conducts a strict commission business, and his fine range affords ample evidence of industry and prompt attention. The most important branch in the trade of this house is in fertilizers and South Carolina phosphates. Mr. Robson does an established business in this line, being among the first of our merchants who introduced the fertilizers, about twenty years ago. The house does an extensive trade, and has maintained so high a standard

ROBSON'S RANGE.

that it has given confidence to the agricultural community in the use of these soil renovators. The Pacific Guano Company, with its extensive works, is connected with this house, and its affairs have been managed with encouraging satisfaction, having increased in demand from fifty tons, in 1866, to thousands of tons in 1874. The popular and reliable

DuPont's Gun-Powder Company, is also successfully managed by this house. . Ludlow's Bagging Company, of Boston, Werk & Co's Candle Factory, of Cincinnati, the best flour mills of Virginia, Georgia, Tennessee, Kentucky and Missouri, have established agencies with this enterprising house. Mr. Robson was a pioneer in introducing Western trade into Charleston. He canvassed the West in 1851. At that time the city received few shipments, but in six years the trade increased to over one hundred thousand barrels of flour and a million bushels of grain. His influence, as a merchant, was felt in turning this affluent tide of trade into the city. He looks forward with hope, that if the resources of a few States now supply sources of wealth to the city, that when the barriers which now obstruct a free flow from the Western. slopes shall be swept away, and the great railroad thoroughfares pour their rich tides through this open gate by the sea, the city will become one of the great centres of commerce. Mr. Robson is chairman of two inportant committees in this branch of trade, one in the Chamber of Commerce on direct trade, and the other on deepening the bar. He entertains the hope of seeing the vessels of all nations enter our beautiful and spacious harbor, affording ample tonnage to transport the rich grain of the West to the crowded markets of Europe. He views Charleston as an important sea-link, the shortest and most direct on the Atlantic coast, in connecting the fertile valleys of the West with the teeming cities of the old world.

Still further up East Bay, on the east side, commencing on Brown's wharf, on the south, and Vendue Range on the north, are the offices of

THE CLYDE STEAMSHIP LINES.

The first arrival of a steamship at Charleston, for coastwise trade, to carry two thousand five hundred bales of cotton, occurred in January, 1870, being the steamship South Carolina, to run on the New York and Charleston Clyde Line. Many thought it was a "great expectation" scheme, and that this port could not be counted on to furnish full cargoes; but now, that years have passed since that first voyage, and the Georgia, with a capacity of two thousand eight hundred bales of cotton, has been added to the line, with a regular departure from each port once a week, it is apparent that the mammoth steamship was what Charleston wanted, combined with a draft of water which permitted entrance and exit even at mean low tide. It was thus demonstrated that, instead of indulging in vague aspirations for deep water at some obscure point on the coast, where cotton fields and wide stretches of marsh spread out to view, an established port, with population, banks, warehouses, merchants in correspondence with all parts of the world, and capacious docks, cotton presses, piers, and a well sheltered harbor, possessed advantages which controlled business to such an extent that in spite of the wasteful experiments, intended to cut off trade from Charleston, the statistics of the port show

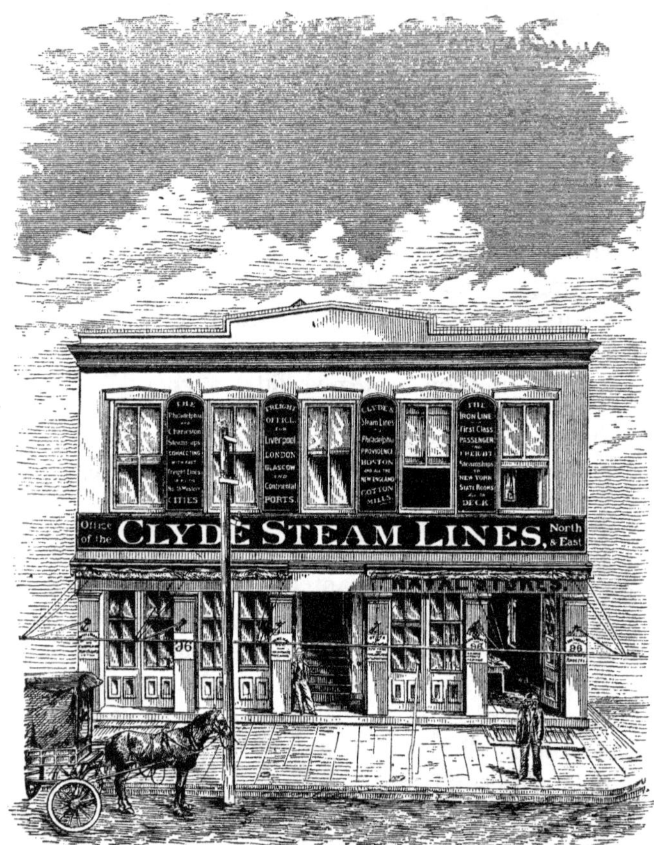

Photo. by Barnard. *Eng. by Photo. Eng. Co., N. Y.*

THE CLYDE STEAMSHIP LINES.

those annual gains which point unmistakably to the supremacy in the near future which, up to 1860, Charleston always held.

Since the advent of the New York Clyde Line, the Philadelphia and Charleston steamships have passed into the same management, and improved vessels substituted for the smaller and less attractive ones of the former line, and under these advantages, the business has developed and promises a fair success.

The New York Line comprises the Georgia, Captain Crowell, and the South Carolina, Captain Nickerson, with a cotton capacity of eleven thousand bales per month, but these steamships are so thoroughly adapted to the general business of the port that the agents are able to give accommodation to general shipments, and an immense freight tonnage, which has heretofore gone by sail, is now given regular dispatch by the Iron Line. Since the establishment of these steamships, over four hundred thousand bales of cotton, thirty thousand casks rice, one hundred and twenty-five thousand barrels rosin, twenty-five thousand bales manufactured goods, two hundred and fifty thousand packages farm truck, and great quantities of miscellaneous freights figure in their exports. The line is popular with the travelling public as well as with shippers, the saloons and state rooms being all on deck, securing a very thorough ventilation, and the tables are luxuriously supplied.

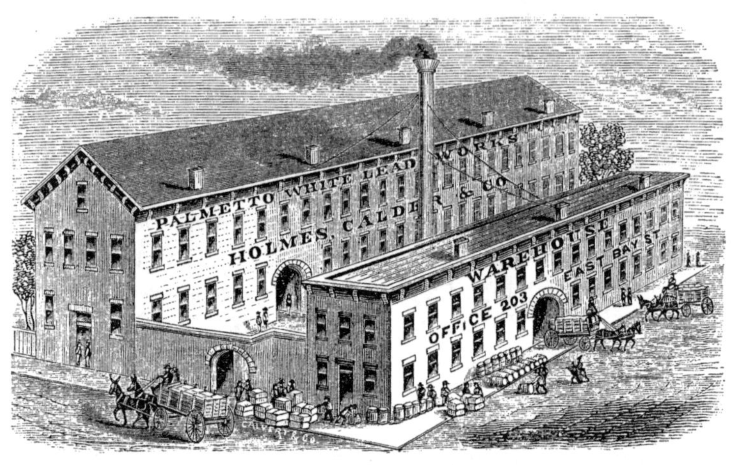

HOLMES, CALDER & CO.

On the west side of East Bay, one door above Cumberland street, is the paint and oil store of Messrs. Holmes, Calder & Co., one of the most enterprising and successful firms in Charleston. They commenced business after the close of the war, young men with small means, and by industry, enterprise, and close attention, they have built up an extensive trade, permeating North and South Carolina, Georgia, Florida, and Alabama. They have established a branch house in Atlanta, for conducting their business in that section more conveniently, and there, as in Charleston, have met with decided success. They manufacture their own white lead, zincs, colors, and putty, at their factory on Philadelphia street, a view of which is here given. They are importers of and dealers in lubricating and paint oils, window glass, and painter's materials; and are, also, agents for Averill's chemical paint, Prince's metallic paint, and India rubber and India rubber belting. Their goods in every line will be found of the best quality and thoroughly reliable, and their prices the lowest the market will afford.

At the foot of Brown's wharf is the office of Pelzer, Rodgers & Co., the largest cotton factors in the city, and the agents of the Atlantic Phosphate Company, and just here it may be as well to say a few words in regard to

THE PHOSPHATE INTEREST.

The history of this new branch of industry in Charleston can not fail to be interesting. We have already mentioned the proportions which it has assumed. These will appear astonishing when we state that ten years ago the value of the deposits around Charleston was, for all practical purposes, unknown. Their existence had been known for many years by scientific men, who were searching among the marl beds, which underlie these deposits, for the fossil remains which are there abundant; these fossils are found in great quantities in the marl beds, and comprise the remains of numerous species of extinct animals, as well as those which still exist. Many of them are very beautiful and very wonderful, bones which must have belonged to animals larger that we have even seen, shark's teeth the size of a man's hand, and remains of creatures which we can hardly conceive of, are to be found in unlimited quantities, and have long been the subjects of inquiry and investigation by paleontologists. Practical farmers also appreciated the marl beds, in furnishing a cheap and easily procured manure for their lands, but these lumps of rock, as they seemed, were disregarded by

PHOSPHATE MINING.

both scientists and farmers, and in fact by the latter were rather regarded as a nuisance, where they cropped out above the surface and interfered with the cultivation of the land. So they remained until 1867, and some time in that year Dr. St. Julien Ravenel received some specimens of the rock from a plantation on Goose Creek, and analyzing it, he was struck with the large quantity of phosphate of lime which it contained.

He presented one or two of the specimens to Dr. N. A. Pratt, who was at that time engaged in a scheme for the erection of some works for the manufacture of sulphuric acid in the neighborhood of the city. Dr. Pratt, upon careful analysis, found that his specimens contained even a larger percentage of phosphate than those analyzed by Dr. Ravenel.

Perceiving the account to which this discovery could be turned, he communicated with Prof. F. S. Holmes, whose accurate knowledge of the geology of the country around made him familiar with the situation and extent of the beds. The two at once proceeded to action; they were liberally assisted by one gentleman in the community, but money was scarce in Charleston, and the few capitalists were unwilling to risk it in such an enterprise. Accordingly they went to Philadelphia, where they obtained the requisite funds, and on their return organized the Charleston Mining and Manufacturing Company.

Meantime Dr. Ravenel, and some others, aware of their action in the matter, organized the Wando Fertilizer Company, and without any assistance from abroad, were making arrangements for the collection and use of the nodules on such a scale as the means at their command would allow. In consequence of the efforts, some small lots were, in the course of the next few months, shipped to the North and Europe, but, naturally, the rock was imperfectly prepared and

Photo. by Barnard. *Eng. by Photo. Eng. Co., N. Y.*

WANDO WORKS.

shipped, and did not at first attract the attention which it deserved. From this small beginning grew the immense business which we now see. The supply of phosphates is practically unlimited, and Charleston can, for many years to come, look upon this as an unfailing source of wealth.

The works of all the companies are finely built and kept in beautiful order, and the various operations of mining, washing, crushing, drying, and shipping the crude rock, as well as the manufacture of it on the spot with a commercial fertilizer, are full of interest.

Through the winter boats frequently run up to these works with excursion parties, and no one who can go ought to fail to see this very striking feature among Charleston industries.

WANDO MINING AND MANUFACTURING COMPANY.

The first company for the manufacture of phosphate rock into a commercial fertilizer, incorporated in this State, was the Wando Mining and Manufacturing Company, which was organized by Mr. John R. Dukes, who was elected its president, and who is fairly entitled to the credit of being the pioneer in the phosphate business. The company was established in 1867, and Mr. Dukes remained in charge of its affairs until October, 1873, when he resigned the presidency and agency of the company, and was succeeded in the former by Geo. E. Gibbon, Esq., and in the latter by Messrs. Witte Bros. Mr. Francis B.

Photo. by Barnard. *Eng. by Photo. Eng. Co., N. Y.*

ETIWAN WORKS.

Hacker, the secretary and treasurer of the company, has held that position from the organization of the company to the present time. Although many other companies have since been formed, not a few of which have altogether failed, the Wando has maintained the reputation which it acquired in its earlier days, and the fertilizers manufactured by it are recognized as among the best on the market. The office of the company is on Atlantic Wharf, in the rear of the post office, but the mines and works, of which a view is here given, are situated on the Ashley river about seven miles from the city limits.

The present officers are: George E. Gibbon, President; Francis B. Hacker, Secretary and Treasurer; Thos. D. Dotterer, Superintendent; Witte Brothers, General Agents. Directors: Geo. E. Gibbon, L. D. Mowry, B. C. Pressley, Thomas P. Smith, Wm. B. Dingle, Charles Kerrison.

ETIWAN COMPANY.

The second company organized was the Charleston Sulphuric Acid and Superphosphate Company, better known as the Etiwan Company—their factory on Cooper River being called the Etiwan Works, from the Indian name of the river. Their fertilizers are also called Etiwan, and, on account of their quality, have always commanded a ready sale, notwithstanding the fact that the price has invariably been kept up to the top of the market. It was the first company to manufacture its own acid, although all

Photo. by Barnard. *Eng. by Photo. Eng. Co., N. Y.*

ATLANTIC WORKS.

the other companies now do the same thing. The company started with a large capital, and put up the most elaborate and complete works, which, at that time, were without a rival. Hon. C. G. Memminger is the president, and Messrs. W. C. Bee & Co. are the general agents, and these gentlemen have held their respective positions from the first, and their management has been completely successful. They have never shunned any necessary expense to make a first-class fertilizer, but have always acted on the principle of keeping their fertilizers invariably up to the high standard which they at first adopted, and the result has been that, notwithstanding the most formidable competition, they have been able to establish a large, safe, and profitable business.

The present officers are: President, Hon. C. G. Memminger; General Agents, Messrs. W. C. Bee & Co.; Superintendent, Caspar A. Chisolm, Esq.; Chemist, W. W. Memminger, M. D. Directors: Hon. C. G. Memminger, Messrs. Robert Adger, E. Horry Frost, W. C. Bee, Caspar A. Chisolm.

ATLANTIC PHOSPHATE COMPANY.

The Atlantic Phosphate Company was organized in May, 1870, and completed its works on the Ashley River in time to introduce its fertilizers in 1871, selling this year a few hundred tons, and has steadily increased its trade, until during the past three years its sales have exceeded that of any other company here. Its reputation is equal to that of the oldest

Photo. by Barnard. Eng. by Photo. Eng. Co., N. Y.

STONO WORKS.

fertilizers now sold in the South, and its productions give perfect satisfaction wherever used. Its management is in the hands of Messrs. Pelzer, Rodgers & Co., whose reputation is a sure guarantee for the standard quality of its productions. The present officers of the company are: Francis J. Pelzer, President; Francis S. Rodgers, Treasurer; W. G. Muckenfuss, Clerk; St. Julien Ravenel, Chemist; W. Lebby, L. D. DeSaussure, W. P. Hall, B. G. Pinckney, Directors.

THE STONO PHOSPHATE COMPANY.

The only other company which we will notice at present is the Stono, which was established about the same time as the Atlantic. This company manufactures a very popular fertilizer, and one that has been found of great service on various kinds of land. Their works are very extensive and complete, and well worthy a visit from strangers. They are situated on the Ashley River, about five miles from the city, and are approached through a magnificent avenue of live oaks, which, in the winter season, are festooned with a vast abundance of grey moss. As can be seen from the engraving, the buildings are large and extensive. There is a large building for the two acid chambers, another for the mill and machinery, and there are others for storehouses, besides the residence of the superintendent and the cottages of the workmen. The works are on the river, and there is a substantial wharf, at which vessels are loaded. The

Photo. by Barnard. *Eng. by Photo. Eng. Co., N. Y.*

CHARLESTON NEWS AND COURIER OFFICE.

situation is just below Accabee, so renowned for its beauty, where the river widens to such an extent as to have the appearance of a lake, the green woods, and cultivated fields, on the other side, forming a charming background to the picture. The officers of this company are: Wm. Ravenel, President; Williams, Black & Williams, Commercial Agents; Dr. St. Julien Ravenel, Chemist; J. B. Keckley, Superintendent at Works. Directors: Wm. Ravenel, Henry Gourdin, Jas. S. Gibbes, Chas. H. Simonton, J. D. Aiken, R. D. Mure, A. Sydney Smith, A. S. Johnston.

THE CHARLESTON NEWS AND COURIER.

This prosperous newspaper was first published, in August 14, 1865, under the name of the Charleston Daily News. Some of the most distinguished men in the State were connected with the News, as regular or occasional writers, but the management of the paper was defective, and, in September, 1867, the concern was sold, at private sale, to Messrs. Riordan, Dawson & Co. Under their management the News rapidly gained strength, which was increased by the subsequent suspension of the Charleston Mercury, which left only the News and the Charleston Courier in the field of journalism in Charleston. In April, 1873, the Charleston Courier was offered for sale, and was bought, at auction, by Messrs. Riordan, Dawson & Co., who consolidated it with the News, under the now familiar name of the News and Courier. The

Charleston Courier was first published in 1803, and had long been one of the most respectable and profitable newspapers in the country. It was sold in order that there might be a settlement of the estates of deceased proprietors. From the time of the consolidation the business career of the News and Courier has been uniformly and remarkably prosperous.

The News and Courier establishment, in Broad street, of which an engraving is given on another page, was formerly the South-western Railroad Bank, and was bought by Messrs. Riordan, Dawson & Co., in 1872. It is massive in structure and imposing in appearance, and, with the two connecting buildings, sweeps back, an entire block, to Elliott street. The business office of the News and Courier is on the lower story of the Broad street building; the editorial rooms are on the second story, and the composing rooms on the third story. In the middle building are the double-cylinder presses, folding and addressing machines, and other machinery, needed for the printing and delivery of the several editions of the paper. To the rear of this is the engine-room. In the large three-story brick building at the corner of Elliott street is the News and Courier Job Printing Office, which is complete in every particular. Between forty and fifty persons are regularly employed in the News and Courier establishment, and it is believed to be the best equipped newspaper office in the South.

Three editions of the News and Courier are published; the daily edition, at ten dollars a year; the tri-weekly edition, at five dollars a year, and the weekly edition, at two dollars a year. These newspapers are taken and read in every part of South Carolina, and wherever interest or affection moves any one to seek news of South Carolina and the South. The News and Courier is the only morning newspaper in Charleston, and is acknowledged to be the leading newspaper in the State.

The News and Courier, while spreading before its readers, every day, a brief history of the events of the world, devotes particular care to the collection, by its corps of reporters and correspondents, of South Carolina and Southern news. In its columns will be found a complete record of whatever passes in the South; and its State and city news is a model of thoroughness and varied interest. In politics the News and Courier is Conservative-Democratic to the backbone; but it is one of the most liberal newspapers in the country. No narrow views will be found in its columns. Its devotion to the South has been often proved; but it is an earnest advocate of peace and reunion on the broad basis of equal rights and mutual respect. Nor has it, in the darkest hours, despaired of South Carolina. Its services, in cheering the public heart, in making known the advantages of Charleston and the progress of her trade, in fighting fraud, and in advocating measures of political, financial, and sanitary reform, have been worth millions to the State.

Photo. by Barnard. *Eng. by Photo. Eng. Co., N. Y.*

CHARLESTON FEMALE SEMINARY.

CHARLESTON FEMALE SEMINARY.

The engraving on the opposite page represents the school building of the Charleston Female Seminary. It is situated at No. 50 St. Philip street, a few doors north of George street, and directly opposite the College of Charleston. It is recessed from the street, has a garden in front, and presents a very attractive appearance. It was built and furnished expressly for the purpose to which it is applied, and thus possesses advantages to be obtained in no other way. The building is so situated as to have windows on all sides, with an open view all around, thus securing perfect ventilation.

It is furnished with the "new American school desks and settees," (Munger's patent, with Allen's opera folding-seat patent) a style of furniture unrivalled in comfort, and elegant in appearance. When desk and seat are folded, less than one foot in width is occupied, leaving ample space, so that the assembly room may readily be converted into a calisthenic hall. Numerous blackboards are set in the wall.

The Charleston Female Seminary was founded in 1870, by Miss Etta A. Kelly, a young lady of this city, who had for several years been vice-principal of the Normal School, and who, in that position, had displayed an ability and fitness for the profession of teaching, that attracted the attention and commanded the confidence of prominent citizens connected with the management of that institution.

Feeling, however, that she could better carry out

Photo. by Barnard. *Eng. by Photo. Eng. Co., N. Y.*

NORMAL SCHOOL.

her views of education in a private school, and being solicited by friends to take charge of their daughters and do so, she resigned her position and started the seminary, in an humble way, in her private residence.

Her success was so great and so immediate, that in a few months she had given out the contract for the erection of the present building. The corner stone was laid June 15th, 1871, and the building formally inaugurated in 1872. Since then the school has been steadily increasing in grade, in numbers, and in influence. It is now divided into a primary and academic department—four years constant attendance in the latter department being required before a pupil can be graduated. During the past year a *pension* was added to the School, and the result was in every way satisfactory, as the boarders all enjoyed excellent health and, at the same time, attained a high degree of proficiency in their studies. Miss Kelly's motto is "*Mens sana in corpore sano.*" She therefore insists upon calisthenics as much as on mathematics. Her success has been simply wonderful, and if it continues, she will be compelled to enlarge her accommodations, and the seminary will become, what Charleston has long needed, a first class female college. The number of scholars the past year was one hundred and forty. The present corps of instructors include ten teachers and a lecturer.

D. F. FLEMING & CO.

One of the most prominent business stands in the city, is that at the north-west corner of Hayne and Church streets, occupied by the well known wholesale boot and shoe house of D. F. Fleming & Co. The business is now forty-three years old, having been first established by Mr. Fleming in 1832. He occupied his present stand in Hayne street in 1838; Mr. Wilson became a member of the firm in 1845, and since then the firm, although occasionally varying in its members, has gone under the name of D. F. Fleming & Co., and has built up an extensive

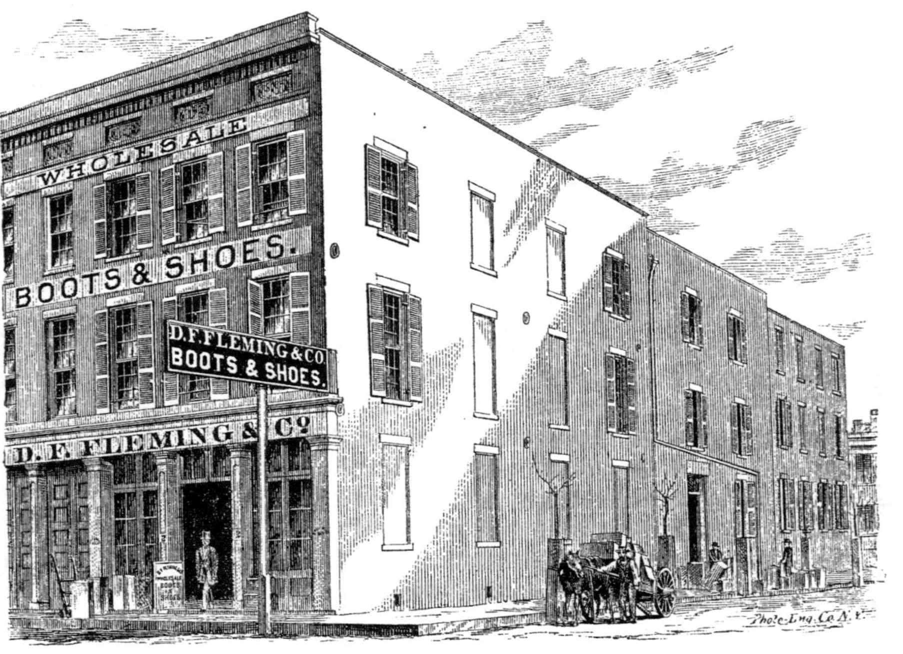

Photo. by Barnard.

Eng. by Photo. Eng. Co., N. Y.

D. F. FLEMING & CO.

trade, winning the confidence and respect of their customers in this and neighboring States, by their uniform courtesy and fair dealing. Their acquaintance and credit with the manufacturers, who know them to be one of the most responsible houses in the South, enable them to purchase goods at the bottom of the market, and, consequently, to sell at prices, and on terms, to suit the trade of the interior. The present members of the firm, each and every one of whom is personally and favorably known to the trade, are Messrs. D. F. Fleming, James M. Wilson, and James Gilfillin.

T. M. BRISTOLL & CO.

The King street store, now owned by the senior member of the firm of T. M. Bristoll & Co., was, after the great disastrous fire of 1838, immediately rebuilt, and in the fall of 1839, leased by Smith & Bristoll, who removed from the store three doors from Queen street. When the Big Boot store was established in 1832, Mr. Smith shortly afterwards withdrew, leaving T. M. Bristoll at the head, where he has remained up to the present time, with only the interruption of business during the late war. Mr. Bristoll took as a partner Mr. Bowler, who, at his death, was succeeded by E. C. Bridgman, who on account of ill-health, was compelled to withdraw, and was succeeded by Mr. A. S. Brown, who is still a member of the present firm. The Big Boot store was established as a one price first-class boot, shoe

Photo. by Barnard. *Eng. by Photo. Eng. Co., N. Y.*

T. M. BRISTOLL & CO., NO. 250 KING STREET.

and trunk store, and the constant aim has been to preserve that reputation unsullied. The Big Boot store is so well known to old Charlestonians and residents of the surrounding country, as to require no comment, and the engraving which appears on the opposite page will seem like a familiar face.

Immediately after the opening of communication in 1865, the firm was re-organized and augmented to by the entrance of Mr. C. T. Dunham, formerly of that well know and deservedly popular wholesale boot and shoe house, Dunham, Taft & Co. The wholesale business is now conducted at No. 145 Meeting street, opposite Hayne. Retail branch, 250 King street, the following being the copartners: T. M. Bristoll, C. T. Dunham, A. S. Brown, and T. C. Ryan. Being all experienced men in the trade, having ample capital and the best relations with the manufacturers, they are able to keep the very best stock on hand, and to make both prices and terms satisfactory to their numerous customers.

SELL & FOSTER.

This firm, composed of Mr. Edward Emerick Sell and Capt. Charles Foster, is a genuine Southern house, and as Capt. Foster was formerly a member of the old house of Bowen, Foster & Co., they can claim to be the oldest white and fancy goods house in the city. At the time of Lee's surrender, Mr. Sell was on duty in the medical department at Chester, S. C., through which place all the sick and wounded

Photo. by Barnard.

Eng. by Photo. Eng. Co., N. Y.

SELL & FOSTER.

were obliged to pass, and there he remained for five months, when being notified by the Federal authorities that the last prisoners had been sent South from Point Lookout, he returned to Charleston, and with Mr. Lengnick, re-established his business, under the name of Lengnick & Sell, in second floor room, twenty by fifty feet, on the west side of Meeting street. On January 1st, 1866, they removed to the corner of Hayne and Meeting, and on January 1st, 1868, to the present establishment, 27 Hayne street. Here they occupy the entire building, four stories high, each floor twenty by one hundred feet. The lower floor is their main store, where are displayed, in great variety, notions of all sorts and kinds. One of the features of this floor is the array of clocks, in which they do a large trade. The second story is devoted to white goods and ribbons, and the stock, in quality and variety, is unsurpassed in the South. The third floor is devoted to millinery, and here can be seen the manufacture of those delicate bits of head gear, destined to become the crowning glory of beauty in all parts of North Carolina, South Carolina, Georgia, and Florida. In the fourth story are stored an immense number of bandboxes and other articles required in the trade, and here also manufacturing is carried on. The whole establishment possesses interest for the curious and will repay a visit from strangers.

Photo. by Barnard *Eng. by Photo. Eng. Co., N. Y.*

TOALE'S FACTORY.

OUR FACTORIES AND MACHINE SHOPS.

Since the war more particular attention has been paid in Charleston to industrial pursuits and the mechanic arts, and several large establishments in various branches of manufacture have been founded. Of these we will proceed to notice a few of the most prominent. On the opposite page we give a view of the new planing mill, door, sash, and blind factory, and lumber yards of Mr. P. P. Toale. Mr. Toale commenced the manufacture of doors, sashes and blinds, immediately after the war, on a small scale, and has gradually increased his business until it has reached its present mammoth proportions. He recently purchased the elegant mill site at the foot of Broad and Beaufain streets, and has erected thereon a commodious factory and building, forty by one hundred and eighty feet, two stories high, with adjoining engine and boiler house, office, stables, etc. The site is an especially desirable one, containing eleven acres of lot and timber pond, located in the very centre of the lumber trade. Here we find added to the former business that of working our native yellow pine for this and foreign markets, together with a general lumber trade. Of the building, the entire lower floor, and more than half the second, is occupied by machinery of the latest and most approved designs, driven by a forty-horse power engine and boiler, with new shafting, pulleys, and hangers throughout. The dry kilns now in course of erection

Photo. by Barnard. *Eng. by Photo. Eng. Co., N. Y.*

RESIDENCE OF JAMES M. EASON, ESQ.

will be an important auxiliary, giving greater dispatch in filling orders, and adding much to the value of the work. As may be inferred, a large portion of the work is done by machinery, yet constant employment is given fifty to sixty workmen, under the supervision of Mr. L. Wetherhorn, one of the most skilled workmen in his line in the State. Among the appliances of the building are fifty-five large fire buckets, and two of the "Great American Fire Extinguishers," of which Mr. T. is general agent. In short, this may be ranked as a first class establishment fully equipped in all in its parts.

The main office and ware-rooms are at Nos. 20 and 22 Hayne street, running through, and forming Nos. 33 and 35 Pinckney street, extensive and commodious sales rooms, in the very heart of our wholesale trade.

The oldest machine shop in the city is that of

J. M. EASON & BROTHER.

It was established about 1825, by Robert Eason, (father of the present proprietor,) and Thomas Dotterer, under the firm name of Eason & Dotterer. The first location of the business was at what is now the south-west corner of Hasel and Concord streets. Mr. Eason shortly withdrew from the firm, and the business was carried on by Mr. Dotterer alone, with great success. He put together the first engine used on the South Carolina Railroad, and afterwards built five or six engines out and out for the same road.

The first engine he built was called the Little Native, and on her trial trip had the honor of bringing in a large English engine that had broken down, as well as the train which the large engine had carried out. The railroad business was one of the inducements for the removal of the machine shops to their present location at the north-east corner of Columbus and Nassau streets. On the death of Mr. Dotterer, his brothers-in-law, Messrs. James M. Eason, and T. D. Eason, took charge of the business, and it has since continued under the name of J. M. Eason & Brother; although Mr. J. M. Eason alone survives. The largest contract ever undertaken by J. M. Eason & Brother was, probably, the cleaning out of Beach Channel. The contract was signed May 26th, 1856, the firm agreeing to remove one hundred and thirty-three thousand cubic yards of earth from the channel, and the city promising to pay sixty cents per each cubic yard removed. The work was performed under the supervision of the United States Inspector, and the money only paid on his certificate that the work had actually been done. The work was commenced February 24th, 1857, and finished September 16th, 1858. If it had not been for the war, the city would have reaped the fruits of this labor, but as it was, it was all thrown away.

During the war this firm did a great deal of work for the Confederate Government, building torpedo boats, making propellers for vessels, etc., etc. They now manufacture boilers, steam engines, rice mills, rice threshers, cotton presses, cotton gins, ditching machines, and in short, everything that can be turned out by first-class iron works.

TAYLOR IRON WORKS MANUFACTURING COMPANY.

The establishment of this company is probably the largest of the kind in the Southern States. It occupies almost an entire square, being bounded on the north by East Bay, on the south by Pritchard street, and on the west by Concord street, and extending on the north almost to Hasel street. At the corner of East Bay and Pritchard streets has just been erected a large two story warehouse, for the sale of engines, machinery, belting, etc., in short everything which is manufactured by the company, or that can be imported to more advantage. The centre of the grounds is occupied by the principal machine shop, an immense building containing an endless variety of machinery. There are also a number of sheds for casting and boiler making, and a huge iron tank has been placed on the top of a great wooden tower, and is kept filled with water, and is supplied with pipes to throw the water on any part of the works in case of fire. The president of the company, Mr. John F. Taylor, after whom the company was named, and who originally established the works, is the inventor of "Taylor's Direct Acting Steam and Hydraulic Press," now recognized as the best for compressing cotton, and in use in all the large cotton depots.

Among the articles manufactured and sold by the company, are house fronts, marine, stationary and

Photo. by Barnard. *Eng. by Photo. Eng. Co., N. Y.*

TAYLOR IRON WORKS.

portable steam engines, boilers, tanks, hoisting engines, saw mills, rice threshers and mills of every description, shaftings, pulleys and gearing, iron fronts for buildings, castings of every kind in iron or brass, forgings of all descriptions, phosphate washers, phosphate and ore crushers, steam fittings, wrought iron pipe, sheet rubber and gaskets, water and steam gauges, belting, packing, etc., Taylor's patent direct acting steam and hydraulic presses, Samuel J. Chapman's patent trap strainer, for bilge pumps, bilge injections, etc. Boilers can be taken from or put on board steamers, by the crane on their wharf.

The officers of the company are: John F. Taylor, president; Fred. Brotherhood, superintendent; James S. Simons, secretary; W. E. Breese, treasurer; H. Buist, solicitor. Directors: G. W. Williams, D. C. Ebaugh, F. J. Pelzer, C. A. Chisolm, J. C. Mallonee, D. H. Harvey.

DEVEREUXS' MILLS.

The engraving on the following page represents the steam power works of Messrs. Devereux & Brother, architects, builders, and manufacturers of builders' supplies in wood. These works are conveniently situated, on Ashley River, within the city limits, and are the only works in Charleston, and, we believe, in all the South, where frame buildings are prepared to order, and shipped to any point. Doors, sashes, blinds, mouldings, and other builders' supplies in wood are furnished from these works on short notice.

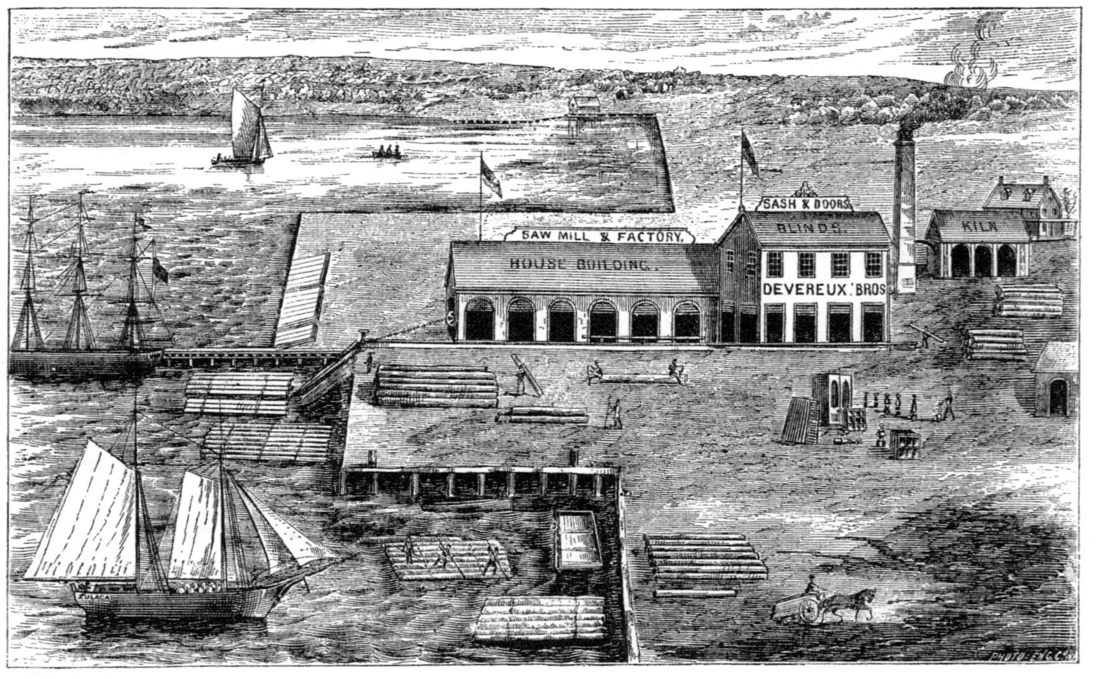

Photo. by Barnard. Eng. by Photo. Eng. Co., N. Y.

DEVEREUXS' MILLS.

They offer to the South the advantages of a first-class builders' manufacturing establishment.

These mills are the fruit of the industry and enterprise of this firm, the senior members of which (J. H. and J. W. Devereux) commenced business in 1857. After the war, their brothers, N. F. and P. Devereux, also practical mechanics, joined them. They have steadily increased their operations and business facilities. Some of the finest modern structures in the city attest their taste and skill. Of the buildings represented in this volume, the new German Church and Masonic Temple were designed and erected by them. The Chamber of Commerce, also represented in this volume, and other buildings, were remodelled by them. The Academy of Music, however, alone gave an opportunity for the display of the artistic skill foreshadowed in the work of art by the senior member of the firm while yet an apprentice, of which we find the following notice in the *Courier* of November 27, 1856: "In the group of statuary are several busts by young Devereux, whose early promise gives token of the sculptor by intuition."

The Academy is a gem, and it alone fulfills the high expectation of the foregoing extract.

THE DOOR, SASH AND BLIND FACTORY OF GEO. S. HACKER

is well known throughout this State for its first-class work. It is situated in King street, opposite Cannon street, and the rear of the factory is directly on the yard of the South Carolina Railroad, thus having

Photo. by Barnard. Eng. by Photo. Eng. Co., N. Y

HACKER'S WORKS.

unusual facilities for transportation. Mr. Hacker is a native South Carolinian, and a man well known and appreciated by his fellow citizens. He has been engaged in this branch of manufacture for many years, and is thoroughly posted in all its details. The engraving on the opposite page gives but an inadequate idea of the extent of the factory, as only the front of the main building is seen. This building is much larger than the picture would lead one to suppose, while another building, including the boiler and engine, and a part of the machinery is entirely concealed from view. The warerooms in front are used for storing finished work, and glazing, and painting. Mr. Hacker's is the oldest established door, sash and blind factory in the city, having been first established in 1842. It now counts its customers in North Carolina, South Carolina, Georgia, and Florida.

JOHN S. FAIRLY & CO.

This firm occupies the extensive buildings Nos. 37 Hayne street, and 70 Market street. The engraving (on the following page) represents the Hayne street front. The building is four stories high, is the fifth from the corner of Meeting street, and is in the centre of the jobbing trade of the city.

The firm possesses the experience and capital requisite to enable it to supply the trade in its lines of business with goods suitable to the wants of the city and country, and at prices as low as those of any northern city.

Photo. by Barnard. *Eng. by Photo. Eng. Co., N. Y.*

JOHN S. FAIRLY & CO., No. 37 HAYNE STREET.

Mr. Fairly was connected with the house of Shepherd, McCreery & Co., first as book-keeper, and afterwards as salesman, from 1852 to 1856. When the firm of Marshall, Burge & Co. was organized, he became a partner of that house and so continued until the outbreak of the war, when he entered the Confederate service. Finding himself without means at the close of the war, it was not until in the autumn of 1866, he obtained a copartner with capital, and again embarked in the line of business of his old firm, viz: wholesale dealers in hosiery, white goods, fancy goods and notions, at 37 Hayne street, where he has continued to conduct it successfully under the present firm name.

In January, 1872, Mr. McBurney, of Hyatt, McBurney & Co., former owners and occupants of the buildings, (whose old sign board reburnished is prominent in the engraving,) took an interest in the firm; and the trade of the house requiring greater facilities for the conduct of its increasing business, arrangements were made to occupy the entire premises running through from Hayne to Market street.

It is one of the best appointed establishments of its kind in the whole country, and merits the attention and patronage of all dealers in that line in this section of country.

SILCOX'S FURNITURE WAREROOMS.

The extensive warerooms, of which a view is given on the next page, are occupied by the firm of D. H. Silcox & Son, the largest dealers in furniture in Charleston. The building was erected expressly for

Photo. by Barnard. *Eng. by Photo. Eng. Co., N. Y.*

SILCOX'S FURNITURE WAREROOMS.

the furniture business, by Mr. Wm. Enston, but at his death, in 1860, was bought by the present firm. Mr. D. H. Silcox commenced business at the corner diagonally opposite the present stand, in 1838, and carried it on continuously and successfully until his death, in 1874. Some years previous to his death, he had associated his son, Mr. D. S. Silcox, in partnership with himself, and that gentleman has continued to carry on the business in the old name. The firm has always made a specialty of fine furniture, and taken pride in dealing in first-class goods and doing first-class work, and the houses of some of the wealthiest people of the city have been furnished by them, in a manner at once creditable to their taste and to their resources. As said before, the building was built expressly for the furniture trade, and is admirably adapted to the purpose. There are three stories, each consisting of one large room, without division or partition, the ceilings being supported by rows of iron columns. On the first floor may be seen such chairs, bureaus, bedsteads, washstands, icehouses, etc., as are most commonly sold, and require to be oftenest exhibited. In the second story are costly sets of drawingroom and bedroom furniture, while in the third, common furniture is compactly put away in great quantities.

FOGARTIE'S BOOK COMPANY.

The depository of the Fogartie Book Company, is eligibly situated, next door to the famous old stand of Russell, whose name was familiar as household

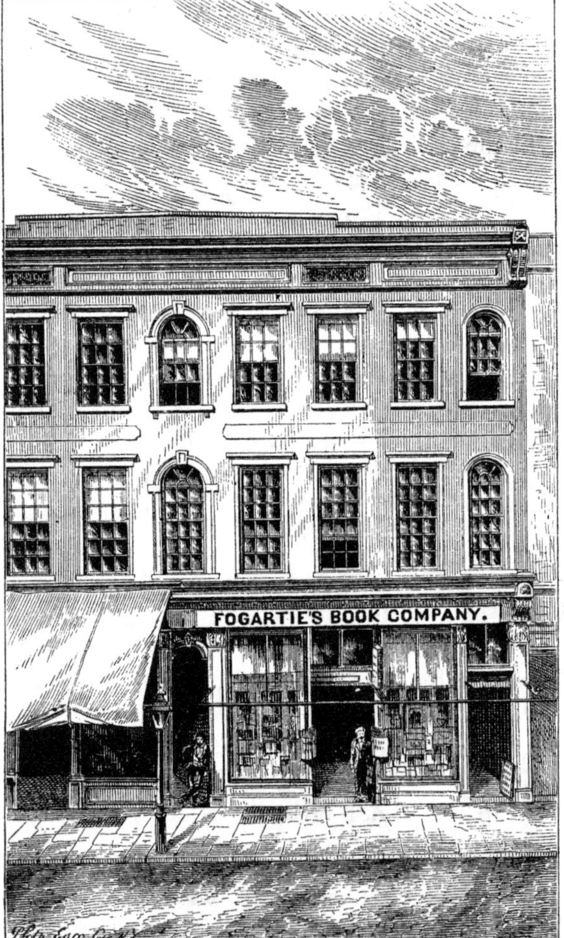

Photo. by Barnard. *Eng. by Photo. Eng. Co., N. Y.*

FOGARTIE'S BOOK COMPANY.

words in the last generation. The building occupied by the Book Company is a large and commodious one, on the first floor of which is their celebrated bookstore. As we pause, and glance into the store, we see its shelves, and tables well filled with an extensive stock of English and American literature; everything looks so cosy and inviting, we feel that we must walk in. As we take our seat at one of the numerous tables, on which are spread the latest periodicals, we notice that not only have the literati made this place their resort, as one after another of the clergy and learned profession enter, with the air of men who are at home, but that the rising generation are following in their footsteps in coming here to procure the necessary adjuncts of school life.

Mr. F. is the oldest bookseller by many years in Charleston; this veteran bibliopole began his career in this business about thirty-five years ago; his novitiate was passed in the establishment in Chalmers street, which was known as the depository of the Sunday-school Union Tract and Bible Societies, and conducted by D. W. Harrison. We next find Mr. F. in the bookstore of the popular and lamented Beile. After the death of Mr. Beile, he formed a business connection with the well remembered W. R. Babcock, and is the only survivor of W. R. Babcock & Co.

The stranger will find this a quiet, pleasant resort.

The library rooms of the Protestant Episcopal Society are in the same building, and it is also the depository of the Charleston Bible Society.

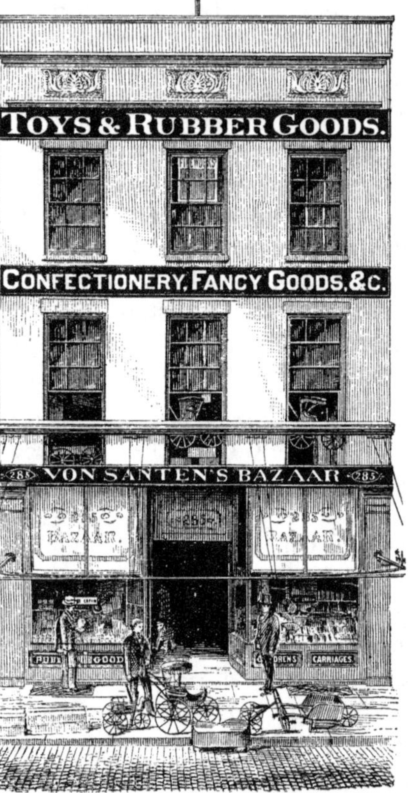

Photo. by Barnard. *Eng. by Photo. Eng. Co., N. Y.*

VON SANTEN'S BAZAAR.

One of the most attractive establishments in the city, for strangers as well as natives, is

VON SANTEN'S BAZAAR,

an engraving of which appears on the opposite page. The proprietor, Mr. Frederick Von Santen, is the right man in the right place, and has a host of friends, who make his bazaar their favorite rendezvous and a source of profit to him, as well as pleasure to themselves. In summer his ice cream saloon is the chosen resort of the young people of both sexes, and in winter his store is sacred to the juveniles as the shrine of Santa Claus. In addition to his retail department, which is so well known to all Charlestonians, and which should always be patronized by tourists, Mr. Von Santen does a large jobbing business with the merchants of the interior, and by making a specialty of his particular line, is able to give great satisfaction. He imports large quantities of foreign fancy goods and toys, and pays particular attention to French confectionery. He also deals in fireworks, dolls, games, and India rubber goods. Any merchant visiting Charleston to purchase goods, will find it greatly to his advantage to examine Mr. Von Santen's large and varied stock.

To travellers this store is important for its extensive stock of stereoscopic views of the city and surrounding country.

Photo. by Barnard. *Eng. by Photo. Eng. Co., N. Y.*

HOLMES' BOOK HOUSE.

HOLMES' BOOK HOUSE.

At the corner of King and Wentworth streets is to be seen one of the landmarks of Charleston, viz: Franklin's Head. This is a sign which has hung at that corner for years, and now, as at first, indicates a first-class bookstore. It is, and has been for fifty years, one of the favorite resorts of the literati of Charleston. It first became famous under Mr. W. R. Babcock, who occupied the stand until 1858. Holmes' Book House, the present establishment, was founded in 1866, by Professor F. S. Holmes, who sold the business in 1873 to his son, A. Baron Holmes, the present proprietor. A large and varied stock of books in every department of literature can always be found here. Collectors in search of old and rare volumes should make it a point to call on Mr. Holmes, who has made a specialty of this department of the business. The very best collection of relics and documents connected with the Confederate war is probably that in his possession.

JEWELRY ESTABLISHMENT OF MR. JAMES ALLAN.

Mr. Allan is himself a practical jeweller, and understands every detail of the business, and to this knowledge is doubtless to be attributed his great success. The interior of his store is artistically arranged, and displays his handsome stock in so alluring a manner, that a customer, especially a lady customer, hardly knows when to leave. Feasting her eyes on costly

Photo. by Barnard *Eng by Photo. Eng. Co., N. Y.*

ALLAN'S JEWELRY STORE.

watches, she tears herself away from them, only to be irresistibly attracted by diamond sets, pearl necklaces, brooches, ear rings, finger rings, studs, buttons, pins, in endless variety and glittering confusion. If her taste is more for solid worth than great display, she has only to cross to the other side of the store, and there she may spend her fortune in silver plate, handsome pitchers, teapots, urns, cake baskets, cups, napkin rings, spoons, fruit knives, etc., which there make a splendid array. To enumerate the clocks, desks, music boxes, opera glasses, and the thousand and one other articles to supply the necessities, or to administer to the luxuries of life, would take more space than can be spared in so small a volume. Suffice it to say that Mr. Allan is the favorite jeweller of some of the richest and most fashionable people in the city, and that he has the happy knack of giving satisfaction to his customers.

Just below Allan's the stranger is at once struck by the umbrellas and big hat which mark the

UMBRELLA AND HAT STORE OF MR. B. JOHNSON.

Mr. Johnson's umbrella business has been established for many years, and the reputation which he has obtained for the durability of his materials and superior quality of his work, has created a demand for his umbrellas, canes, and parasols. He has recently added hats to his other business, and, on the same principle of giving good articles at moderate prices, he is bound to succeed. See next page.

Photo. by Barnard. *Eng. by Photo. Eng. Co., N. Y.*

UMBRELLA AND HAT STORE OF MR. B JOHNSON.

RAILROADS.

No account of the city of Charleston would be complete without some description of the South Carolina Railroad, which is one of its principal institutions, the interest of the city and of the railroad having always been identical. It is the oldest railroad in the United States—the South Carolina Canal and Railroad Company having been chartered in 1827, and the Charleston and Cincinnati Railroad Company in 1835. These two corporations were consolidated in 1844, under the name of the South Carolina Railroad Company. It has always been the leading railroad in South Carolina, and one of the most important roads in the South.

At the present time, the South Carolina Rail Road Company operates under its immediate organization two hundred and forty-three miles of first-class single track, thoroughly equipped in all respects, and fully prepared at all points to meet any emergency in the business of transportation. It has for its local termini, within the limits of its own State, the city of Charleston, the city of Columbia, and the town of Camden, traversing an intermediate territory at once populous, fertile, and prosperous. Its fourth, and western terminus is in the city of Augusta, Ga., and there it connects immediately with the Georgia Railroad, and through it with the entire ramified railroad system of the Western and Gulf States.

At Columbia, S. C., its connections are with all the

lines radiating from that centre, and it especially controls, though under a distinct organization, the management of the road and branches to Greenville, Anderson, Walhalla, Abbeville, and Laurens. The service of transportation on this road of both passengers and freight has always been characterized by the utmost precision, safety and dispatch. The transit of through freight is uninterrupted from the point of shipment to its ultimate destination, the common and mutual interchange of cars between all connecting roads insuring their passage without the breaking of bulk. Through its well systematized forwarding department, all the various business details incident to the service of moving freight are promptly and carefully attended to, and claims of either loss, damage or otherwise, arising out of the same, are invariably made the subjects of special and immediate action.

The South Carolina Railroad is an integral part of the Great Southern Freight Line, and one of its most important links, connecting, as it does, on deep water at the port of Charleston, with the several steamship lines and fleets of sailing vessels, engaged in the carrying trade from and to all the chief Northern and Eastern coast cities.

The steamships composing the lines, from New York particularly, are vessels of the most approved construction, and especially adapted in their draft of water, speed, and safe sea-going qualities to all the requirements of the service. Their trips are generally made each way inside of sixty hours, and shippers by this route rely with confidence upon every possible care and attention being given to the protection of their interests. These ships are likewise provided with admirably appointed and completely ventilated passenger accommodations, and enjoy a very large patronage from the pleasure-seeking as well as the business travelling public. The steamships forming the Philadelphia and Baltimore lines are likewise well built, substantial vessels, possessing all the good qualities requisite to ensure safe carriage, quick trips, and have deservedly won public confidence and support as being among the most reliable carriers on the coast.

The North-Eastern Railroad extends from Charleston to Florence, a station on the Wilmington, Columbia and Augusta Railroad, one hundred and three miles from Charleston, and one hundred and three miles from Wilmington, North Carolina; at this point it connects with the Cheraw and Darlington Railroad.

The Savannah and Charleston Railroad extends to Savannah, Georgia, one hundred and ten miles, via Grahamville.

The Spartanburg and Asheville Railroad commends itself to the merchants of Charleston. This road is a link in the great through line—a national highway, so to speak—destined to connect the cities of Louisville, Cincinnati, St. Louis, Toledo, Indianapolis, Chicago, and San Francisco, with the central South Atlantic port of Charleston. The road runs from Spartanburg, via Asheville, to Wolf Creek, the Western Counties of the Cincinnati, Cumberland Gap, and

Photo. by Barnard. *Eng. by Photo. Eng. Co., N. Y.*

BREAKING GROUND FOR THE SPARTANBURG AND ASHEVILLE RAILROAD.

Charleston Railroad, and will be, for the entire length, one hundred and fifteen miles. Twenty-five miles from Spartanburg, northward, are graded, and work upon the remainder is being pushed forward rapidly. The cost of the entire road will be $2,500,000, of which a very large amount has been subscribed in capital stock, and additions to the same being regularly made by the people of North and South Carolina. Of the road between Asheville and Wolf Creek, included in the one hundred and fifteen miles above alluded to, two-thirds of the grading, the heaviest and most expensive portion of the work, is finished.

The line of road is as follows: from Charleston to Columbia, on the South Carolina Railroad; from Columbia to Spartanburg, on the Spartanburg and Union Railroad; thence by the Spartanburg and Asheville Railroad to Morristown, Tennessee, and on to the principal cities of trade. We would urge the speedy completion of this road upon our merchants, throwing, as it naturally must, the entire grain trade of the West over the shortest and cheapest possible route, necessarily creating a line of foreign steamers for shipment to the old world. The construction of this link opens at once the finest trans-mountain region in the South to the trade of our merchants, from which they have been heretofore cut off by the mountain barriers. The books for subscription to the stock are now open. D. R. Duncan, President; W. K. Blake, Secretary and Treasurer.

Mrs. HOPSON PINCKNEY'S

Boarding and Day School

FOR YOUNG LADIES,

No. 58 HASEL STREET,

CHARLESTON, S. C.

This Institution offers to Parents and Guardians the advantages of a Finishing School for Young Ladies, combined with the comforts of a refined home. Boarding pupils are received into the family of the Principal, and become objects of maternal care. Attention is given to the cultivation of the mind, the affections, and the manners; while the health is promoted by regular exercise. Competent Professors are employed in all the usual branches of useful and ornamental education. For the results of her system, the Principal has the honor to refer to the correspondence of the Patrons of the School.

CORRESPONDENCE.

Hon. W. F. COLCOCK, Gillisonville, S. C.

" From a personal acquaintance of nearly twenty years with your system of education, it affords me unqualified pleasure to say that it has always met my highest approbation in every particular, which is necessary to make not only scholars, but ladies of our daughters."

Hon. T. C. WEATHERLEY, Bennettsville, S. C.

" As a patron of your School, I was well pleased with your discipline, and your method of teaching seemed all that the most exacting could desire."

Chief Justice DUNKIN, Charleston, S. C.

"The experience and observation of several years have satisfied me of your marked ability in the service of instruction, and I fully appreciate the excellent results."

Hon. JAMES SIMONS, Charleston, S. C.

" As a parent, perhaps over-anxious on this point, I do not hesitate to say that I have always rejoiced that my own daughters were so fortunate as to be in a position to avail themselves of your moral and intellectual training."

J. A. McRAE, Esq., Bennettsville, S. C.

" In addition to your efficiency in the school room, I was impressed with the maternal care and solicitude exhibited in the training of the young ladies under your care."

Hon. J. P. REED, Anderson, S. C.

" I am alike satisfied with your system of teaching and with the superiority of your training."

Col. J. L. BLACK, Ridgeway, S. C.

" I have had a daughter two years with Mrs. Pinckney, and I take great pleasure in recommending this as a Finishing School for Young Ladies ; and regard it, in this respect, as far ahead of any Female Institution in the State. The management is superior and the house combines the advantages of a school, with those of a polished home circle."

S. Y. TUPPER, Esq., Charleston, S. C

" It is with satisfaction and gratitude that I cordially commend your method of training, whereby the personal conduct and manners of your pupils are formed ; while equal attention is paid to their intellectual and moral culture, all of which tend to the formation of character. It is very pleasant in our home circle, to hear you frequently referred to as authority for gentle civilities and rules of conduct."

Major FRANZ MELCHERS, Charleston, S C.

"I take great pleasure in recommending your efficient School My daughter has made good progress with you, in all the branches she has studied."

REFERENCES.

HON. W. D. PORTER, Charleston, S. C.
B. BOLLMANN, ESQ., Charleston, S. C.
A. R. TAFT, ESQ., Charleston, S. C.
G. H. INGRAHAM, ESQ., Charleston, S. C.
ED. BARNWELL, ESQ., Charleston, S. C.
DR. W. T. WRAGG, Charleston, S. C.
W. J. BENNETT, ESQ., Charleston, S. C.
REV. W. O. PRENTISS, Charleston, S. C.
W. J. MIDDLETON, ESQ., Charleston, S. C.
JAMES DUNBAR, Barnwell, S. C.
MAJOR CLYBURN, Lancaster, S. C.
J. B. BISSELL, ESQ., Charleston, S. C.
DR. P. PORCHER, Charleston, S. C.
WM. UFFERHARDT, Charleston, S. C.
DR. J. L. DAWSON, Charleston, S. C.
FRANCIS WESTON, ESQ., Pee Dee.
JAMES HEYWARD, ESQ., Charleston, S. C.
W. H. PERRONEAU, ESQ., Charleston, S. C.
H. GOURDIN, ESQ., Charleston, S. C.
R. N. GOURDIN, ESQ., Charleston, S. C.
W. K. RYAN, ESQ., Charleston, S. C.
S. A. WOODS, ESQ., Darlington, S. C.
DR. WILLIAMSON, Darlington, S. C.
T. D. JERVEY, ESQ., Charleston, S. C.
F. J. PELZER, ESQ., Charleston, S. C.
DR. F. PEYRE PORCHER, Charleston, S. C.

TERMS.

The Scholastic year, commencing October 1st, and closing July 31st, is divided into two sessions of five months each.

PER SESSION OF FIVE MONTHS.

English Senior Class		$40 00
English Junior Class		25 00
French		12 to 20 00
German		20 00
Drawing and Painting		20 to 23 00
Music		40 00
Fuel		3 00
Stationery, etc.		3 00
Board	Per Month,	30 00
Washing	Per Month,	2 00
Use of Piano	Per Month,	1 00
Seat in Church	Per Month,	1 00
Bedding, etc.	Per Month,	1 00

No deductions for absence except when caused by sickness.

Vacation, the months of August and September.

Terms, in advance, or one-half in advance, and the balance in the middle of the session.

THE CHARLESTON
CROCKERY
IMPORTING COMPANY.

GEO. W. WILLIAMS & CO.,
PROPRIETORS.

WILLIAM G. WHILDEN,
MANAGER.

EARTHENWARE

Imported Direct from the Potteries to Charleston; also, Goods for Local Trade Packed to Order.

Glassware, Yellow & Rockingham Ware, Pipes, Looking-Glasses,

AND MISCELLANEOUS ARTICLES.

KEY BOX 418. CHARLESTON, S. C.

DRUGS AND MEDICINES.

J. E. TORLAY,

(Successor to Dr. WM. A. SKRINE,)

260 King Street, Charleston, S. C.

Sole Manufacturer of Epping's Compound Fluid Extract of

Sarsaparilla and Queen's Delight,

AND THE CELEBRATED

COLLETON BITTERS.

Country Orders from Physicians and Families solicited and promptly attended to.

EMPORIUM OF FINE ARTS.

CHARLES HICKEY,

DEALER IN

LOOKING GLASSES,

EVERY VARIETY OF MOULDINGS, WINDOW CORNICES,

Photographic Frames, Cord and Tassel Loops, Etc.,

No. 345 KING STREET, above Liberty,

CHARLESTON, S. C.

ENGRAVINGS AND OIL PAINTINGS RENOVATED.

www.ingramcontent.com/pod-product-compliance
Lightning Source LLC
LaVergne TN
LVHW050518100826
845148LV00002B/373

* 9 7 8 1 4 2 5 5 2 0 3 3 5 *